More praise for Urban School Leadership

"Leadership in America's schools and school districts is a critical element in bringing high-quality education to all children in America. Tom Payzant is widely recognized for his stellar work as one of America's top educational leaders. In *Urban School Leadership*, he provides current and aspiring school and school district leaders, school board members, and other education policymakers with answers to key questions they must identify to educate all children to meet high standards—which, in previous times, were expected only of the select few. This important book provides compelling examples of how effective leaders can have hope, see progress, and achieve success for all children in the schools and districts they lead."

—**Richard Riley,** former United States
Secretary of Education

"Tom Payzant is one of the finest urban educators of our generation. Policy makers, practitioners, and parents should all read this book. *Urban School Leadership* is compelling, crisp, and wise—providing a clear path for those dedicated to improving the trajectory of children's lives."

—**Timothy F. C. Knowles,** Executive Director,
Center for Urban School Improvement,
University of Chicago

"Tom Payzant's *Urban School Leadership* is must reading for anyone interested in the landscape of urban public education in America. It constitutes a one-stop, comprehensive picture of a truly American institution that is challenged on numerous fronts today more than ever before."

—**Beverly Hall,** Superintendent,
Atlanta Public Schools

D0365958

"Tom Payzant's unparalleled experience as an educational leader is clearly reflected in *Urban School Leadership*. He describes the increasingly complex landscape today's district and school leaders need to understand in order to shape urban systems capable of educating all students. Astute and practical!"

—**Naomi Cooperman, Ed.D.,** Director of
Curriculum and Instruction,
Teaching Matters, Inc.

The Jossey-Bass
Education Series

THE JOSSEY-BASS

Leadership Library in Education

•

Andy Hargreaves

Consulting Editor

THE JOSSEY-BASS LEADERSHIP LIBRARY IN EDUCATION is a distinctive series of original, accessible, and concise books designed to address some of the most important challenges facing educational leaders. Its authors are respected thinkers in the field who bring practical wisdom and fresh insight to emerging and enduring issues in educational leadership. Packed with significant research, rich examples, and cutting-edge ideas, these books will help both novice and veteran leaders understand their practice more deeply, and make schools better places to learn and work.

ANDY HARGREAVES is the Thomas More Brennan Chair in Education in the Lynch School of Education at Boston College. He is the author of numerous books on culture, change, and leadership in education.

For current and forthcoming titles in the series, please see the last pages of this book.

Tom Payzant

Urban School Leadership

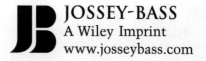
JOSSEY-BASS
A Wiley Imprint
www.josseybass.com

Published by Jossey-Bass
A Wiley Imprint
989 Market Street, San Francisco, CA 94103-1741—www.josseybass.com

Jossey-Bass books and products are available through most bookstores. To contact Jossey-Bass directly call our Customer Care Department within the U.S. at 800-956-7739, outside the U.S. at 317-572-3986, or fax 317-572-4002.

Jossey-Bass also publishes its books in a variety of electronic formats. Some content that appears in print may not be available in electronic books.

Library of Congress Cataloging-in-Publication Data

Payzant, Thomas W.
  Urban school leadership / by Thomas W. Payzant.
      p.   cm.—(The Jossey-Bass leadership library in education)
    Includes index.
    ISBN 978-0-7879-8621-6 (pbk.) ISBN 978-0-4709-1835-7 (ebk.)
    ISBN 978-0-4709-1836-4 (ebk.) ISBN 978-0-4709-1837-1 (ebk.)
      1. Education, Urban.   2. Educational leadership.   3. School management and organization.   I. Title.
  LC5115.P39   2010
  371.2009173'2—dc22

                                                                    2010023121

Printed in the United States of America
FIRST EDITION
PB Printing   10 9 8 7 6 5 4 3 2 1

Contents

The Authors

Tom Payzant is currently a professor of practice at the Harvard Graduate School of Education. The focus of his work is leadership and systemic reform in urban school districts and schools. He served as superintendent of the Boston Public Schools from 1995 until his retirement in 2006. For most of the 1980s, Payzant was superintendent of the San Diego public schools, then became Assistant Secretary for Elementary and Secondary Education during the Clinton administration. In 1998, he was named Massachusetts Superintendent of the Year. He also received the McGraw Prize for his leadership of the San Diego school system from 1982 through 1993. Throughout his career Dr. Payzant has kept abreast of the professional and research literature and contributed to it regularly. His essays, book chapters, book prefaces, and book reviews have been directed to both professional educators and policy makers.

Janice Jackson is an independent education consultant with a focus on leadership and organizational change in public schools and districts, equity strategies, teaching and learning, teachers' and principals' professional identity, and reflective judgment of principals and teachers. Her last roles were Lecturer on Education at the Harvard Graduate School of Education and the Senior Associate on the Wallace funded Executive Leadership Program for Educators. Dr. Jackson is also a faculty member in the Leadership for Change Program in the Carroll School of Management at Boston College. She entered higher education after serving as the Deputy Superintendent for the Boston Public Schools. During the first term of the Clinton Administration she served as Deputy Assistant Secretary for Elementary and Secondary Education.

Urban School Leadership

Our Urban Schools

Leaders are shaped in part by the context in which they lead. By *context* I mean the different environments and settings wherein leaders engage with others. Successful leaders are often able to effect changes in context, which are prerequisites for altering what is and creating the conditions for what could be. Whether results are positive or negative depends on many factors. Leaders may be able to control some factors; others defy their influence. Followers will often disagree with leaders as to what should be sustained and what should be changed, why change is necessary, what the pace of change should be, or whether change should occur at all. Understanding context is essential to principals' and superintendents' ability to develop strategies for leading change and improvement in urban schools and school districts.

The focus of this book is leadership in America's urban schools and school districts, particularly the principals and superintendents who, with teachers and other staff, educate millions of children in elementary, middle, and high schools across America. The quality of instruction in classrooms and the effectiveness of leadership in schools and school districts are the most important variables that schools can influence to improve student achievement. I believe that there are both generic characteristics of effective leadership and particular characteristics that are defined by the purposes of the organizations or institutions leaders lead, and by the contexts in which these organizations function. I will use both my general experience with leadership and my own work and experience serving as a superintendent in five school districts— Springfield Township, Pennsylvania; Eugene, Oregon; Oklahoma

City; San Diego; and, most recently, Boston—to convey to aspiring and current school and school district leaders the importance of this work, the challenges they face in doing it, and how it is possible to make a positive difference in the lives of the students they serve.

The Challenge of Urban Scale

The United States has about fourteen thousand public school districts, ninety-five thousand public schools, and three million teachers serving fifty million students. There are still one-room schools serving students of various ages in some rural areas, and there are megaplex buildings serving thousands of students in some cities. Between those two extremes, there are many variations in the organization and structure of public schools; and within larger county and urban school districts, it is not unusual to find schools that are organized with a variety of structures defined by grade levels. With the emergence of public charter schools in recent years, the debate about optimal school size and how best to organize and structure schools has new energy. In states with many small school districts, the call for consolidation to increase efficiency and reduce costs still creates significant political risks for elected officials who are challenging the value of local control, which most communities in America embrace. Local school boards and district leaders face similar tough decisions to close or consolidate schools, particularly where enrollment is declining and budget cuts are endemic.

Conversely, in many urban school districts, particularly at the high school level, there is a trend toward breaking up large comprehensive high schools and creating small schools or small learning communities within them, or starting new small schools housed in a variety of facilities and locations. Educators continue to struggle to honor the logic of creating space for schools to serve their educational purpose. However, the availability of existing space or the cost of new space and resources available to secure it usually become the controlling variables. How to provide sufficient space in schools and classrooms to educate all children is a fundamental systemic challenge and requires strategies that will produce solutions at scale.

New pressures affect urban school districts that are experiencing declining enrollment in addition to the added challenge of making the severe budget cuts that resulted from the recession that began in 2007 and continued through 2010 with no clear end in sight. Many states have had to cut funding to local school districts. Most school districts allocate 80 percent or more of their budgets for salaries and benefits. Many had no choice but to increase class size and cut central office and teaching positions. Those with declining enrollment were forced to consolidate or close schools, even though the politics of doing so were difficult.

The goal of graduating all students with high school diplomas that certify they are ready without remediation to continue their education and prepare for careers creates high expectations for urban district and school leaders who are addressing the additional challenges of doing more with fewer resources. Classrooms must have capable teachers whose instruction will inspire and support each student to meet the high standards that only some students were expected to meet in the past. In many urban school districts, 50 percent of new teachers leave during the first five years of their employment. Retaining effective teachers is essential. Principals must ensure that the teachers in every classroom provide high-quality instruction for each student and receive the support they need to continue to improve their skills. Staff who guide from the middle levels of the central office must understand and execute their support roles as they help school leaders develop their instructional leadership and management skills, as well as hold them accountable for the steady increase in student achievement. The superintendent must set the leadership expectations for all and model the leadership behavior expected of central office and school leaders. Achieving these outcomes also requires systemic strategies that shape the work for improving student achievement throughout the school district. Leaders must meet these challenges to take best practices to scale in school districts and schools.

No longer is success in urban schools defined by a few more students in a classroom achieving at high levels, by a few more classrooms in a school meeting higher standards, or by a few more good schools in a school district. A good school system is not the same as a good system of schools. A good urban school system may have some or even many good schools and aggregate data that suggest it is beating the odds and educating most students well. However, the details embedded in the aggregate data can shine a spotlight on gaps in achievement among different groups of students, which educators must understand and address to ensure that all students are learning and meeting high standards.

> A good urban school system may have some or even many good schools and aggregate data that suggest it is beating the odds and educating most students well.

The standards-based framework for school reform was created in the late 1980s and began to gain traction in the early 1990s. It was a radical idea: the expectation was for all students to be educated to high standards that would provide them with access to opportunity beyond high school. The framework had four clear components: standards in each subject for what students should know and be able to do; access for both teachers and learners to a rigorous curriculum aligned with the standards; support for teachers to engage in continuous improvement of their instruction; and data from both formative and summative assessments of student achievement, with the expectation that some data would be used for accountability purposes, and other data would be used by teachers to determine when it was necessary to modify the curriculum or their teaching strategies during the school year and to differentiate instruction. From the outset, the framework was designed with the intent of creating alignment among the components, and coherence for school leaders, teachers, and students.

However, with a commitment to standards-based reform, the goal of having a good school system usually falls short of the mark of ensuring that all children achieve at high levels. It takes time to convince school and district staff that steady growth and improvement for all students are possible. Evidence is essential, and good school systems showcase schools and classrooms where student achievement is improving and achievement gaps are narrowing. Compelling data are more effective in changing beliefs than is emotional rhetoric. The difference in a good system of schools is its effectiveness in taking improvement to scale. In a good system of schools, the commitment is to improve all schools in the system, consistent with the expectation that school leaders and teachers will improve instruction for all students in all classrooms. The goal for the superintendent is to lead a system of schools with a commitment to improve all schools and not have a legacy marked by the improvement of only a few schools. The goal for central office people should be the same whether leadership touches only a few schools where they have responsibilities or serves all schools in the system.

The challenges of reaching the goals of having all children meet rigorous curriculum standards and achieve at high levels and of closing the achievement gaps defined by race, class, disabilities, gender, and native language exist for all leaders with diversity among their students, regardless of the size of school or school district, its location or demographics. However, the challenges for urban district and school leaders and increasingly for leaders in the urban-suburban fringe areas with rapidly changing demographics are unique because of the complexity and scale of the districts and schools they lead.

Most urban school districts have some outstanding schools that serve most students very well. They have the achievement results to demonstrate their success, and if there are opportunities for parent choice in their districts, these schools can point to the number of parents on their waiting lists as validation of their success. What about the other schools and all the other children? The leadership challenge is to take the strategies for improvement within classrooms and within schools to scale: to ensure that all students stay in school, receive quality teaching, learn at high levels, and have what is necessary to access opportunity when they graduate.

In the following sections, I explore further the major issues facing urban district and school leaders, what they need to know and be able to do, and how they can effectively help those they lead ensure that all students will learn and succeed.

Globalization and Technology

Trying to decide whether globalization preceded dramatic advances in technology or the rapid development of technology led to globalization is a debate about the chicken and the egg. It is reasonably clear that one will not succeed without the other, and leaders in all sectors must understand the impact of both. President Obama and Arne Duncan, the secretary of education, have set a goal of reauthorizing the Elementary and Secondary Education Act in 2010. If passed, the new legislation would replace the controversial No Child Left Behind Act that preceded it. One of the expectations in the administration's proposal is that states would be required to develop more rigorous standards that students will be expected to meet to graduate from high school ready for college. The proposed goal is for all students to reach this target by 2020.

Although the debate about the wide variation in the rigor of standards in the fifty states has become more transparent, there is little support for the federal government's creating national standards. In 2010, forty-eight states took the unprecedented step to work together to develop common standards in English language arts and mathematics. There is increasing recognition that the standards developed independently by each of the fifty states in the past and the new common standards that may be adopted by many will not be nearly as rigorous as the international standards set by many of the industrialized nations in the world with whom the United States competes.

America has relied for many years on its creativity and commitment to innovation to maintain its leadership position in world trade. But it is no longer alone. Many countries are competing successfully in the international markets for new ideas, services, and products. Ironically, most American colleges and universities are educating international students in undergraduate and graduate programs that develop their skills and enable them to return to their own countries with new insights about creativity and innovation that will help their countries become more entrepreneurial and successful in a flat, competitive, globalized world.

Another dynamic of globalization in recent years has been guest worker programs and offshore worker programs. Many countries bring in workers from other countries to fill jobs requiring low skills and paying low wages, which their own workers will not do. Others bring in workers to fill jobs demanding higher-level skills. During the last few decades, U.S. corporations have been going offshore to find highly educated workers who will perform well in jobs requiring sophisticated skills, at lower wages than highly skilled American workers demand. Globalization has also resulted in a decline in manufacturing in the United States because products manufactured in other nations can be produced at lower cost. The dramatic advances in technology have changed how work is done, and the continuing advances in technology have created a world where competition still exists, but the distribution of intellectual capital is an important driver of interdependence. Globalization and the dramatic advances in technology are beginning to have an impact on how we in America think about teaching and learning, but we are still struggling to embrace new approaches and let go of some of our traditional and outdated ones.

Globalization is flattening the world, reducing isolation, and creating opportunities for both competition and collaboration that demand a willingness to reach beyond our borders and cross international boundaries. Most large U.S. cities have new immigrants arriving from all parts of the world, and as was the case in previous periods in America's history, the public schools are the institutions educating the newcomers. Urban public schools have a unique opportunity to become the setting where both newcomers and those students who are third-, fourth-, and fifth-generation Americans learn to respect and embrace diversity, work independently and in groups, acquire a second language, engage in lifelong learning, and become creative and innovative to succeed in the twenty-first century.

Advances in technology have loosened restrictions on where work is done. Location is no longer a primary factor for many jobs, and distance learning offers virtual educational settings. America's strengths still are grounded in the creativity and innovations well-educated people can produce, yet we are slow to change our ways of organizing opportunities for learning in most school districts and schools. We must ratchet up our expectations for what students need to know and be able to do, shake off a one-size-fits-all approach to teaching and learning, and acknowledge that the students in America's elementary and secondary schools are the first generation to be born into a digital world.

When I began my work as superintendent of the Boston Public Schools (BPS) in fall 1995, the mayor, Thomas Menino, was beginning to think about what the city would need to do to improve its infrastructure and how technology would be an important component of the plan. He made the commitment to work with the district to capture federal E-rate funding and other sources to fund the wiring of all 125 schools; ours was the first large urban public school district in the nation to do so. (I remember being in a meeting where someone said that in the future there would be wireless systems and that perhaps we should wait before making the big investment required to provide all schools with access to computers.) Initially the computers were clustered in labs, and later they migrated to classrooms. The professional development challenges were significant, and one of the incentives to attract motivated teachers to become leaders in their schools was to provide them with laptop computers once they successfully completed extensive training. Few educators could imagine the rapidity of the change that would occur in the next ten years and how quickly the "digital natives" who appeared in their classrooms were more savvy than many of the adults in adapting to ways to access information.

International competition and the globalization that spawns it are much more transparent in the high-tech era, bolstered by technology that has exponentially increased access to information and data and has enabled leaders to make decisions in real time. Knowing what to do when you don't know is one of the skills that well-educated people and leaders develop as they think, explore options, and solve problems. Watching students who are digital natives troubleshoot a glitch in their computer, video game, cell phone, or iPod seems to confirm that their thinking and problem-solving skills can be more intuitive and multidimensional than those of previous generations. But these students also become frustrated when quick solutions are not easily accessible. They must not only learn that mental agility, flexibility, the passion for continuous learning, and the passion to discover, innovate, and create are important but also develop the patience to stay focused, persistent, and realistic about the time and effort required to demonstrate high-quality and lasting results—in a culture where expectations of instant gratification are reinforced through easy Internet access and other advances in technology. Moreover, as leaders in education, we must not ignore the lessons of history, which

As leaders in education, we must not ignore the lessons of history.

demonstrate that discovery resulting in innovation and positive change rarely occurs quickly or by chance. Rather it is the product of continuous effort, a disciplined work ethic, and an acceptance of deferred gratification.

Equity and Ambiguity

Equity is a word that is often misunderstood. The *American Heritage Dictionary of the English Language* defines it as "the state, quality, or ideal of being just, impartial, and fair" or as "something that is just, impartial, and fair." Justice, impartiality, and fairness are subject to wide interpretation. Equity is rarely achieved if all we do is simply provide everyone with the same—that is, equal—resources. It is not just, impartial, or fair when some children arrive at kindergarten without the benefit of a high-quality, developmentally appropriate preschool education and with vocabularies half the size (or less) of those who have spent their first four years of life with widespread exposure to thousands of words and good books. In these situations, the achievement gap develops early and can quickly widen once children are in school without the additional support necessary to narrow the gap. It is likely that additional resources will be required to meet the equity standard, and when they are scarce, the reallocation of resources may be necessary; tensions will arise because many both inside and outside of schools see "equal" as what defines just, impartial, or fair. It is not.

Leaders in school districts and schools must be skilled in leading courageous conversations with adults and students about race, class, and equity, and what it will take to create opportunities for all students to graduate from high school ready without remediation for postsecondary education of some kind. Effective leaders are clear and transparent about their beliefs and core values and about what they expect those whom they lead to do to ensure that equitable decisions are made in school district offices, schools, and classrooms. Leaders who attempt to hold others to higher standards than they are prepared to reach will not be credible. Effective leaders model the behavior they expect of others and are consistent in aligning what they say and what they do.

In America, the gaps between the "haves" and "have nots" continue to widen. In 2007 the minimum wage was raised for the first time in ten years. Between 2007 and 2010 it has been raised twice. The dramatic shift in the economy that began in 2007 and created the "Great Recession" resulted in hundreds of thousands of jobs lost, homes foreclosed, bailouts for Wall Street firms, and billions of dollars in stimulus funds provided by the federal government to stem the losses and provide relief to states where tax revenues were shrinking. Cities and towns that rely on state funding were also seeing local revenue shrink because of declining property values, business closures, and job losses. By late spring 2010, the key economic indicators showed that there were some states where the recession was ending and new jobs were being created. However, many school districts, cities, and towns that used one-time stimulus money to mitigate the loss of some jobs and services were hoping not to have two to three more years of budget cuts. Some were more cautious in how they spent their stimulus money, knowing that it is dangerous to use one-time funding for continuing costs. This is an unprecedented climate in which superintendents and principals, particularly in urban and rural areas, must lead school districts and schools populated by students from families struggling to find jobs, affordable places to live, and money to provide for their children. These conditions create additional challenges for district and school leaders as they struggle to distribute shrinking resources equitably.

Is there equal opportunity for children in urban public school districts and schools? Is there equity? Is there adequacy? The glib answer to these questions is no, not in many cities compared to neighboring suburban public schools and other communities with additional resources. It is clear that the challenges presented by these realities cannot be addressed and resolved by cities and schools alone. Also critical are affordable housing, adult education, jobs, universal preschool education, health services, and better aligned federal, state, and local funding streams to support them.

It is clear that federal, state, and local governments have roles and responsibilities for public education, which include setting policy, allocating resources, and holding school districts and schools accountable for results. Then why is there ambiguity? The 1954 Supreme Court case *Brown* v. *Board of Education* and the civil rights movement of the 1960s placed the issues of equal opportunity and equity on the doorsteps of the public schools, first in the South and then by the 1970s in the North. The progression of expectations set by the courts began with *Brown's* reversal of the doctrine of "separate but equal" and continued with court decisions in the 1970s and 1980s that required equality of opportunity, and with legislation in the late 1980s and 1990s that set the standard for equality of outcomes defined by student achievement. Although the expectations of the courts were clear, fifty different states were responsible for setting public education policy and choosing their own timelines for establishing and funding their policies. The disparities in the amount of money states provide to school districts and how it is allocated within states have resulted in lawsuits filed in many states asking courts to address the issue of the adequacy of funding necessary to provide an equitable education for all students. The Elementary and Secondary Education Act, passed in 1965 by the House and Senate and signed by President Johnson, did provide incentives and funding for school districts with high concentrations of low-income students to address the issue of equity.

There was no ambiguity about the targeting of the federal dollars. Differentiated student needs required differentiated allocation of resources to meet the goal of participating on a level playing field. With prodding from the courts, the federal government has also provided resources for students with disabilities and English language learners. However, the initial commitment to provide funds to support these students has not come close to meeting the targets included in the federal policies. Annually there is uncertainty, which leads to ambiguity as states and school districts struggle to prepare their budgets and meet timelines for their adoption without a clear understanding of what federal allocations will be. The federal government has addressed this problem to some extent by making forward funding decisions that are better aligned with state and school district schedules for budget adoption.

We cannot forget that public education exists to serve the common good in a democracy; however, those who resist paying taxes to support their local public schools seem to have done so. A democracy cannot thrive unless all of its children are educated to a standard that enables them to reach their full potential, access opportunity, and become responsible citizens. Achieving equity for all students is a unique challenge for urban school districts and schools. These schools must narrow and close achievement gaps. No one can ignore issues of race and class, and leaders must become skilled in initiating the difficult conversations about the inequalities, convincing those they lead that the schools can address them and make a positive difference in the lives of all children. Examples of best practices at schools where achievement gaps are being narrowed will be addressed in Chapters Three and Five.

Competition, Choice, and Public Perception of Schools

In most school districts in America, the school a student attends is determined by where he or she resides. Attendance boundaries are drawn to include the projected number of students who live in the geographic area, and children are expected to attend the school located there. The challenge is to draw the boundaries so that the number of seats in the school will equal not only the number of students who live in the area when the boundaries are set but also the number that will be in the area in the years ahead as demographics change and families with or without children move in and out of the neighborhood. Among the most challenging decisions that school boards face are those with regard to changing attendance boundaries, closing schools, and acquiring sites for new schools. District and school leaders can expect to be caught up in the controversies that surround these decisions.

There is a reciprocal relationship between schools and neighborhoods, which is manifested in different ways. New schools are built when new housing is built and new neighborhoods are developed. When new homes and new schools are opened, there is excitement about the opportunity to begin anew. The newness creates a sense of optimism that it will be a good school. In time its reputation will be shaped and judged by the educators, students, families, and community members who are engaged with the school. The opportunities for success are enormous. With family and community support, the school leaders, teachers, and staff can set high expectations for all students attending the school to achieve at high levels and for families and community members to become partners in the effort.

For decades, which public school a child went to was usually determined by where the family lived, and those with the means often chose where they lived based on the local school's reputation. In the 1960s, court-ordered desegregation began to change that pattern. Students were assigned and bussed to schools outside their neighborhoods, and parents had no say in the matter. Although home address still defines school assignment in most school districts in America, more urban and some other school districts have chosen plans that give parents the opportunity to select schools other than their neighborhood school.

The results of desegregation were mixed. In some schools, caring school leaders, teachers, parents, and community people worked together to knock down the barriers of race and class and create a healthy, productive school climate. Elsewhere, less effort was made. For some students and their families, the opportunities provided by better schools outweighed the difficulties. For many, however, the cold and even hostile reception they received shattered their hopes.

In the 1970s, the magnet school became one of the more popular strategies to bring students of different races together. The idea was that schools would attract black and white families equally, by virtue of each school's special curriculum or program focus, resulting in voluntary integration. Innovative school district and school leaders saw these schools as a proactive, positive way to embrace diversity, bring students from different neighborhoods together, and use the carrot of a quality education in an integrated setting as a way to market the schools and advance integration. This was a significant departure and offered a positive alternative that became one of the anchors for the choice options that have since emerged.

During the 1990s, the charter school movement began to gain traction, drawing on some of the characteristics and attraction of the magnet schools. Parents who are dissatisfied with their district schools have eagerly embraced the charter school option. The big difference between magnet and charter schools is the autonomy they are granted. Charter policy in some states requires the state to issue the charter. Other states grant local school boards authority to approve in-district charter schools. Typically the charters are granted for four to five years. Many use a lottery system to select students. Most charter schools are located in urban areas. The demographics in most align pretty well with those of the urban school districts. However, often the percentage of special education students and English language learners in charter schools falls below that of the local school district.

By 2010, districts have had ten or more years of experience with charter schools. Some schools have failed and been closed. Others have been very successful and continue to have long waiting lists of applicants. And the academic performance of students in many charter schools mirrors the range of student achievement in local school districts. The local newspapers publish the results of the state tests in English language arts and mathematics for all districts in the state and all charter schools.

Federal, state, and local school district policies focused on accountability for results and increasing interest in school choice have increased the demand for data and their use in decision making. Parents and the general public expect transparency and want information about how their public schools are doing and how they compare with others. It is clear that district and school leaders must be knowledgeable about data—they must embrace them and use them to understand what is and is not working. With a smile on my face, I say to those who fear data that data are our friends. We must know what parents, staff, students, and the general public think about their school districts and schools. The annual national public opinion poll sponsored by the *Phi Delta Kappan* provides information on what Americans think about public schools and how they grade them. Grades reflecting satisfaction with the classroom were highest; grades for the school, school district, state, and nation followed in descending order. Similar polls designed to measure the public's view of other institutions produce similar results; for example, respondents express lower levels of satisfaction with Congress, yet tend to say "My representative or senator is fine," which may explain why so many incumbents are returned to office for another term. In my experience as superintendent in urban districts where there is school choice, parents tend to rate their schools more highly than parents in those districts without school choice.

For example, BPS has a comprehensive choice system. The school district is divided into three geographic zones, each with about thirty-five elementary, K–8, and middle schools. There

> *We must know what parents, staff, students, and the general public think about their school districts and schools.*

are three 7–12 schools, which serve students citywide who meet entrance requirements. Parents have citywide choice for all other high schools. Parents also have a choice of charter schools that are approved by the state and located in Boston. (During my ten years as superintendent in Boston, forty-two hundred students left the school district to enroll in charter schools. However, each year a hundred or more students who left BPS to enroll in charters returned to the district.) An agreement reached in 1994 between the Boston Teachers Union and BPS led to the creation of pilot schools that have many of the autonomies that the state-approved charter schools have. The first three pilot schools opened in the 1995–96 school year, my first year as superintendent. They have created competition with the charter schools and have made a positive difference in keeping families in the school district who would otherwise consider charter schools or other options for their children. The number of pilot schools had expanded to twenty-two in Boston by the 2009–10 school year, and several school districts in other regions of the United States have started pilot schools. Boston parents also have an additional choice to consider, Metco, a forty-year-old program that serves three thousand Boston students in two dozen suburban school districts.

Most of the public school districts in America do not have as expansive a choice system as Boston and some other urban school districts. The norm is for only those children who reside within the attendance area to be served by the particular school. If intradistrict transfers are allowed, they are an exception. Some states allow choice through interdistrict transfers, but space constraints in the sending or receiving school districts (or both) tend to limit participation.

Socioeconomic status has a powerful impact on what choices and access families have and the public's perception of urban schools. Families who do not have a choice because they live within a geographic boundary that defines who attends the school may still be satisfied if they believe their neighborhood school is good. Families who do not have options and perceive their neighborhood schools as lacking are, appropriately, dissatisfied and demand options for their children to attend better schools in other neighborhoods.

The public perception of school districts and schools is not shaped solely by parents, who have immediate concerns about what schools their children will attend. During my career as an educator, which spans more than forty years, I have witnessed the rapid growth of advocacy groups with special interests. They exist in both public and private sectors to affect federal, state, and local policy and allocation of resources to align with the interests of their members. They have come to be known as stakeholders. They are present in Washington DC, in state capitals, at school board meetings in public school districts, and at school site council meetings in public schools, advocating for policies their members champion and for the resources they need to support their causes. Many of these groups have become quite sophisticated at shaping public opinion.

School boards, superintendents, and principals must be advocates for all children and are challenged by the advocates demanding that the programs they support be given priority for funding. In my experience, there has never been enough money to support all the programs that advocates would like school districts and schools to provide. Often the school district and schools are judged on the basis of whether or not the advocates are successful in convincing school leadership to agree. School boards tend to try to satisfy every advocacy group, but there are rarely sufficient resources to do so. The costs of programs to serve special education students, English language learners, and gifted and talented students, or that offer world languages, art, music, and physical education, continue to increase; the core subjects of English

> *School boards, superintendents, and principals must be advocates for all children.*

language arts and mathematics require more time and attention to meet federal and state accountability requirements. Science and social studies are also important core subjects. Narrowing the curriculum is a poor idea and not acceptable as a strategy for yielding dramatic increases in high school graduation rates.

The leadership challenge for district and school leaders is to understand the importance of clarifying priorities. Every program is a top priority for its supporters, and public opinion often is shaped by the desires of those who do not have school-age children. Often they are reflecting on their own school experience from many years ago and believe that the basic subjects are essential but others less so, and that the annual requests for increases in funding to support the public schools are excessive and unsustainable. For leaders the choices are difficult, particularly when constituents expect equal treatment in allocation of resources and do not understand that the equitable allocation of resources must be the standard, based on what is best for students and not what may be desired by adults who have a variety of special interests. In this age of accountability, it is also important to understand that if school districts and schools attempt to implement too many programs, covering too much in a superficial way, they may lose sight of the importance of going deep to ensure students' understanding of curriculum content and how to apply what is learned. Building the capacity for principals and teachers to go deep with quality instruction in a manageable number of priority areas will be necessary to reach the goal of graduating all students from high school prepared for some postsecondary education. This is what it will take to change the perception of the American public about its schools: demonstrating that they are capable of delivering on the promise of educating all students—not just a select few—to high standards.

The public's perception is that too many urban schools are dysfunctional and incapable of teaching all students the necessary skills. All too often this perception undermines efforts to enhance the public's understanding that public education exists to serve the common good and that all citizens have responsibility for supporting public schools in their towns and cities. This view can be changed as urban superintendents and principals build the capacity in their districts and schools to support all students and provide opportunities for them to achieve at the high levels necessary to access opportunity beyond high school. American cities will not prosper in the twenty-first century unless their schools graduate students prepared for postsecondary education and able to meet the challenging international benchmarks that high school graduates in other countries are reaching.

The twenty-first century began with the courts still involved with student assignment plans and deciding whether race could be used as a factor in determining how the plans were designed and carried out. The charter school movement developed traction, making their impact felt as they recruited students, leaving empty seats behind and taking money with them. Urban district and school leaders who take for granted that the districts and schools they lead will be unaffected by competition from an increasing number of educational choices and options will not be leaders for long. There are choice plans in increasing numbers of urban school districts that enable students to go to schools outside their neighborhoods. They are no longer limited by the boundaries of their neighborhood attendance areas, but issues of equity may create new limits if parents are expected to provide transportation for their children to attend their schools of choice but cannot afford to do so.

> *The challenge for urban district and school leaders is to understand how to lead in an environment where competition is valued and not feared.*

The challenge for urban district and school leaders is to understand how to create and lead in an environment where competition is valued and not feared, families and students have more not fewer options, the markets determine which schools are over- or underchosen, the entrepreneurial spirit is embraced rather than rejected, and issues of equity are resolved and do not create barriers that limit access.

Human Capital

Perhaps it sounds glib to say so, but in school districts and schools, people are the most valuable resource. In school districts, 80 percent or more of the annual budget is allocated to salaries and benefits for educators and support staff. In schools, it usually is 95 percent. Clearly, success in reaching the goal of educating all students to high standards depends on school districts' and schools' developing and carrying out policies that result in getting the best people to do the work and supporting them in improving what they do. Simply opening the schoolhouse door and expecting qualified applicants for teaching, leadership, and other staff positions to walk in is not realistic. School districts and schools must develop and execute comprehensive plans to recruit, hire, assign, induct, support, and retain the best-qualified people to lead and teach in urban districts and schools.

The landscape for attracting good people to the education profession has changed dramatically during the past fifty years in the following ways:

• Prior to the 1960s, women and minorities had few options for professional careers in business, law, engineering, medicine, and other higher-status professions. Teaching, nursing, and social work were the major career options for women. Leadership positions—superintendents and senior staff in school districts, and principals in schools—generally belonged to males.

• In the last quarter of the twentieth century, the barriers of gender and race began to crumble, albeit slowly at first and more rapidly as steady increases in the number of school-age children raised demand for more schools and teachers. Salaries and benefits in many districts improved, driven in part by collective bargaining contracts in states with public employee collective bargaining legislation. Many colleges and universities were expanding teacher training programs.

Simultaneously, changes were occurring in U.S. public schools. The student population was increasingly diverse, court orders for integrating schools in Boston and some other cities set goals for hiring teachers of color, and new waves of immigration presented new teaching challenges. America's urban public schools had always been the institutions that accepted the responsibility for educating immigrant children, and it was difficult to anticipate how rapidly the patterns of immigration would change after the Vietnam War and continue through the early years of the twenty-first century.

- The number of racial and ethnic groups continues to increase even more rapidly in the twenty-first century in cities and their urban ring areas, and the increasing diversity in language and culture within racial and ethnic groups is also significant. For example, Boston, a midsize urban school district, has experienced dramatic growth in the number of students who must be taught English; currently, more than eighty different native languages are represented.

The increasing diversity of students in urban districts and schools requires leaders to think differently about their human capital strategies and plan for diversifying their staffs in a competitive climate where the demand exceeds the supply. One strategy is for large urban school districts to develop their own programs for teachers and school leaders.

- American public schools since the 1970s have been required to serve most students with disabilities. As recently as the 1950s and 1960s, only those students with what are now considered mild disabilities were served in public schools, but they were often not in special education programs. When I taught history at a junior high school in Tacoma, Washington, in the early 1960s, I spent my last class period every day with twenty-five students with mild or moderate disabilities. No special education certification was required, and I had no training or experience working with students with special needs. I am sure I learned more from that experience than my students with special needs learned from me. I learned the importance of understanding the needs of each student and of not only teaching the subject content but also teaching each student as an individual. In those days, there was much less attention paid to specialization in teacher training, although there are still too many teachers, particularly in secondary schools, who are teaching one or more courses outside their content areas.

As a superintendent in Oklahoma City in 1979, I was required to take a special education course at a local university to qualify for my certification credential. It was soon after the U.S. Congress passed the first major legislation that set forth the requirements for serving students with disabilities in local school districts and schools. I was more familiar with the legislation than the person teaching the certification course. Through the years, the teacher training programs for special education teachers have improved significantly. But in many areas the demand still exceeds the supply.

From the early 1980s to the early 1990s, students with special needs made up 12 percent of the school population. That percentage has remained constant through the years and still is the national average. It was difficult to recruit certified special education teachers at the outset, but the state college and university systems did respond to growing demand by creating programs that met increasingly challenging state certification requirements. New federal legislation set higher standards for ensuring that the rights of students with disabilities were met by states and school districts.

- When I began my work as superintendent in Boston in 1995, I was surprised to learn that 22 percent of the students were in special education programs (the national average was 12 percent), and that close to 22 percent of the school district budget was allocated for special education. Many other larger urban school districts were spending much less on special education because they had a smaller percentage of students with disabilities. I also learned that more than nine hundred special education students were in private day or residential schools with per-pupil costs ranging from $25,000 to $80,000 per student, depending on the severity of the disability. I hired a talented new director of special education, who suggested that we open new day programs in our Boston schools that would better meet the needs of many of the students who had been placed in private day schools. There was resistance from some parents, but we were able to prove that the quality of the school district programs was better than that of what was offered in the private schools, and over several years we cut the number of students in private placements by almost half and saved the school district millions of dollars.

It took federal legislation and court cases to eliminate the inequities that existed in too many school districts and to ensure that all students with special needs would receive the services and supports to which they were entitled. Advances in research have produced new knowledge about disabilities and how to meet the needs of children with disabilities, many of whom are capable of meeting the same high standards that all other children are expected to meet.

The demand for special education teachers continues to be greater than the supply and is one of the major human capital issues facing urban districts and schools.

- Science and mathematics are also areas where the demand for public school teachers exceeds supply. Advances in technology have increased demand for employees with strong backgrounds in math and science. Some school districts have created incentive programs with differentiated compensation packages to enhance their recruitment of teachers in these hard-to-fill fields.

• When benchmarked against practices in other industrialized nations that are competing with America in the global economy, entry-level salaries for teachers in other nations often compare more favorably with those in other professions than they do in the United States. Teachers in many of these countries are in the top third of the classes graduating with university degrees. Teachers are highly respected and have higher status as professionals in these countries. In America, many public school teachers come from the middle and bottom third of college and university graduates. However, programs such as the New Teacher Project, residency programs, and Teach for America are recruiting high-achieving college graduates to their teacher preparation programs.

In March 2010, the U.S. secretary of education released a blueprint setting forth the major policy issues to be addressed in the reauthorization of the Elementary and Secondary Education Act. The Obama administration is very interested in promoting innovation, change, and improvement in America's schools. Competitive federal grants with substantial funding will be awarded to those who present the most compelling and practical proposals. The blueprint also proposes funding for leadership training and development of teachers and principals, recognizing the need to develop incentives to attract candidates to teaching and leadership positions in public school districts and schools. The administration is also supporting the continuation of funding for competitive grants to school districts that are willing to design and implement performance pay systems.

What can urban school districts and schools do to address their unique human capital challenges? How and by whom should teachers be trained? What should the rewards and incentives be? What must change in the way urban school districts and schools are organized to attract top candidates to the profession? How do urban school districts make sure they have their most successful teachers in the schools where children have the greatest needs? What kinds of career ladders can be created for teachers and other educators? What will it take to recruit, hire, assign, induct, support, and retain a talented, diverse, and dedicated group of educators? These are the unique human capital challenges for school district and school leaders that will be addressed in the following chapters.

School and District Reform

The history of school reform movements in the United States goes back to at least the early twentieth century. At that time, it was primarily educators spearheading the efforts, but more recently the courts; federal, state, and local governments; businesspeople; educators; and members of the general public have also become drivers of school reform. For example, the Obama administration is submitting its 2010 proposals for the reauthorization of the Elementary and Secondary Education Act based on the goal of having all students graduate from high school ready for college or careers. Whatever changes are made in the legislation will affect state and local school board policy and set expectations for change and improvement in school districts and schools. The expectation is that these changes will build on the standards-based reform movement that has been gaining traction during the last twenty years.

The starting point in the late 1980s was not so different from what has occurred periodically in America among educators, policymakers, and citizens at the local community level—that is, a review of what students in public schools should know and be able to do in each subject area and at each grade level. What was different was the expanding role of the federal government in requiring states to define the standards for what students should learn and to develop annual assessments to determine student achievement outcomes.

The catalyst for change was the recognition that a high school diploma was not sufficient to prepare students for employment that would yield compensation necessary for a middle-class standard of living. Projections for lifetime earnings confirmed that earning potential increased significantly with each year of education completed. Job opportunities for high school dropouts have been declining except in sectors with low-skill, low-wage jobs.

Educators and the public are recognizing the increasing necessity of ensuring that all students graduate from high school ready for some postsecondary education. Anything less will narrow or eliminate the opportunity for meeting the standards required in high-skill, high-wage jobs. This is not the first time in our history that tracking practices (college bound, general education, vocational education) have been questioned and debated. The report *A Nation at Risk*, issued in 1983, raised questions about the "rising tide of mediocrity," high school graduation requirements, and the necessity to make them more rigorous if American students were going to compete with other high school graduates around the world.

The standards-based movement might not have gained traction had American education policymakers framed the discussion about high school graduation requirements in the traditional way—determining the number of courses in each subject required for a high school diploma, using measures of time spent to determine eligibility for course credits, and tracking students into leveled courses on the basis of measures of intelligence. Traditionally these practices left wide discretion to local school districts, schools, and classroom teachers to determine what content was included in courses and what requirements students had to meet to pass the course and earn a unit of credit toward graduation.

For example, Massachusetts and two other states have been recognized as having the most rigorous standards among the fifty states. The Massachusetts Comprehensive Assessment System (MCAS)—the state's end-of-year tests in English language arts, mathematics, and science—has been recognized as the most rigorous state assessment with the smallest gap of any state (5 percent) between the proficiency standard on the National Assessment of Educational Progress and the state assessment. The MCAS has about 40 percent open response items on the tests, including a long essay based on a prompt, answers to reading comprehension questions, and explanations of how the student solves mathematics problems.

This chapter has addressed the context for developing effective leadership in urban schools and school districts. It introduced the challenges leaders face in urban schools and the opportunities they have to make a positive difference in the education of all students. Innovation and change are the precursors for improvement in student achievement and narrowing achievement gaps. The quality of instruction in every classroom and leadership in each school are the most critical levers for improving student performance. Standards-based reform provides the framework for teaching and learning and sets a high bar for all students to meet high standards.

2

The Legal, Political, and Fiscal Landscape

The roots of local politics in America go deep. For many who aspire to higher office, the journey begins with election to local school boards, city or town councils, and county boards of supervisors. Ambition often leads these elected officials to seek positions in state legislatures or state executive office positions, such as attorney general, lieutenant governor, or governor. And of course the next step for a few could be to run for Congress or the U.S. Senate. When in his first term President Clinton nominated me for the position of assistant secretary for elementary and secondary education in the U.S. Department of Education, I had to prepare for my confirmation by visiting senators in their offices. I was not surprised to learn that some had served in Congress first before running for the Senate. However, several were pleased to tell me about their first political campaigns, which led to seats on their local school boards.

This chapter addresses the leadership challenges school and district leaders encounter as they work with a variety of formal and informal governance structures across the legal, political, and fiscal landscape. Roles and responsibilities and how leaders deal with them will be the focus, highlighting similarities and differences between advisory boards and public school districts' charter school or pilot school boards. Congress and state legislatures, the United States Department of Education, and state boards and departments of education each have policymaking roles that affect school and district governance and leadership. The political skills leaders must develop, and examples of how to apply them, are also an important focus of this chapter.

Governance Structures

The majority of school districts in the United States are governed by school boards, whose members are residents of school districts whose boundaries are often the same as the local town or city boundaries. They are parents, businesspeople, workers of all kinds, retired residents, and others who are invested and interested in helping govern the local public school districts or in seizing the opportunity to begin careers as elected officials. They often focus their campaigns on what they want to sustain or change when they as board members have a chance to shape school district policy. These school boards set districts policies and make many decisions that affect what happens in school districts and schools. Their most important tasks are to select, work with, and evaluate the superintendent. They also make policy decisions; review, deliberate, and approve the annual school budget; and vote on the recommendations presented by the superintendent, such as district goals, a strategic plan, curriculum and programs, personnel appointments, and priorities for contract negotiations (if their state has public employee collective bargaining statutes and school districts are required to negotiate with unions representing employee groups).

School board is the designation for the governing body in all but a few states. In Massachusetts, for example, the governing boards are called *school committees*. Usually members serve for four-year terms, and the terms are staggered. Size of district does not necessarily align with the number of board members. In San Diego, the largest district I led as superintendent, I had five elected board members; in my smallest district, in suburban Philadelphia, I had nine board members; and in the other three districts, there were seven members.

Mayoral control is a relatively new approach to governance; it has gained some traction primarily in urban school districts, such as Boston, Chicago, Cleveland, New York, Philadelphia, and Washington DC. In each of these cities, the mayor is involved in appointing the superintendent or, in the case of New York and Washington DC, the chancellor. I am often asked which model, an elected board or an appointed board, is better. Having worked with each, I've found that the relationship between the board and the superintendent is the most critical variable in both models. Of course the relationship between the mayor and superintendent is also critical in districts where the mayor appoints members to the school board.

Continuity of service and leadership is also a critical variable, assuming that the quality of the people serving is high. For several decades, the average tenure of urban school superintendents has been three years or less. Churn in school boards often is driven by voter dissatisfaction with incumbents who fall short of expectations. Once elected to the board, a new majority with a different policy direction may seize the opportunity to select a new superintendent and shift the policy focus of the school district. Depending on the context and the direction the new board wants to take, there can be positive or negative outcomes.

Disruptive strategies may be necessary to generate change and improvement and, if the results make a positive difference for the students, may prove to be worthwhile. However, if there is a lot of churn and therefore little continuity among the members of the board and its leadership, the risk increases for discontinuity in the policies that shape what occurs in schools, how school leaders and teachers will view their work, and what the impact will be for students and families.

Disruptive strategies may be necessary to generate change and improvement.

For example, a culture of impatience is reinforced by lack of evidence that the new curriculum or program is yielding significant improvement in student achievement in two or three years; the pressure to try something new increases, accompanied by high expectations for rapid improvement.

However, usually it is shortsighted to shift to a new curriculum if there have not been appropriate and sufficient strategies implemented to build the capacity of the principals and teachers who must lead the work in schools and classrooms. Fidelity of implementation is a critical variable in determining whether a new curriculum will live up to its billing. For example, when a school district selects a new math curriculum for all elementary schools that aligns with the state's and district's mathematics standards and assessments, all who teach mathematics are expected to follow the designated curriculum. Teachers may alter somewhat the pacing of units based on the needs of students. However, fidelity of implementation means covering the content and ensuring that all students understand it. Leaders of school boards, school districts, schools, and classrooms must act accordingly.

The politics of education are still lively in many local communities in America. In addition to electing school boards in most cities and towns, citizens often vote for tax overrides to generate additional funding for their local schools, or vote in bond elections authorizing bond financing to cover the costs of building new schools and to fund the costs of major capital projects, such as building additions to or renovating schools. When the voters reject these proposals, the school district is not able to move forward with the projects until there is another election. Superintendents and school boards often must modify the proposals to gain the necessary support from the community.

When I served as superintendent of schools in Eugene during the 1970s, school boards in Oregon had to approve the school district's operating budget, which was then put on the ballot for voters in the community to decide the outcome. The school district had been trying for years to convince the voters to approve a budget that included funding for public school kindergarten programs. To ensure a positive vote for the school district budget, the kindergarten proposal was listed as a separate item on the ballot. For many years the budget passed, although not always the first time it was presented to the voters. The kindergarten program was rejected. During my first budget cycle as superintendent, I proposed to the board a single ballot item with inclusion of the kindergarten program in the budget. The electorate was split. Many were upset that there was no longer the opportunity to vote on kindergarten as a separate issue. Others embraced the logic of not giving line-item veto power to the voters because they expected the elected school board to set policy for the school district. The budget was defeated by a margin of three to two. The school board agreed to submit the budget for a second time; the margin widened, with the dissenters defeating the proposal by a margin of two to one. The school board and I decided to make a third attempt, which further polarized the community but resulted in approval of the budget, which included the kindergarten program. After a very close vote, a recount, and an unsuccessful court challenge by opponents, the budget including kindergarten was approved by the slim margin of thirteen votes.

Those who participated in that election learned the compelling lesson that in a democracy every vote counts. It also was the first high-stakes experience in my career as a superintendent where taking the risk as a leader to do what was right for children made a huge difference. Without the determination of a majority on the school board to risk a third election, it would have taken several more years to provide the opportunity for all students in Eugene—not just those who were fortunate enough to be in families that could afford the tuition for a private-school program—to experience kindergarten. It took several years for the opponents of the kindergarten program and those who were angry about controversial reassignments of school principals (which I made with school board support) to elect a majority on the school board who were clear during their campaigns that they did not support the current superintendent.

Our youngest daughter was a student in the first kindergarten class in Eugene, which of course led opponents to suggest that my reason for pushing the program in Eugene was self-serving. Thirteen years later, I was superintendent in San Diego, and Eugene's first class of kindergarten students was graduating from high school. One of the editorial writers at the *Eugene Register Guard*, who had been one of my toughest critics, contacted me by phone and said, "I am sending you a copy of a piece I am writing about the high school graduating class, which was the first class to have access to public kindergarten. I want you to know that your leadership made a difference and that you were right to start public kindergartens in Eugene."

The state and federal governments have roles in school governance and significant influence in shaping policy for school districts and schools, though most of the responsibility for setting education policy rests with the states. Since the passage of the No Child Left Behind Act in 2002, the impact of federal education policy on schools has become more pronounced. The work of district and school leaders is heavily shaped by those who create and govern policy at the federal, state, and local levels of government. An essential role of district and school leaders is to help policymakers form sensible policies that will lead to change and improvement in school districts and schools. It's also necessary to clearly understand the roles and responsibilities of the school boards and other state and local elected officials as well as community leaders, and to develop a collaborative partnership in which all parties agree on the terms and division of these responsibilities.

Governance works differently in dependent and independent school districts and in charter schools. Independent school districts have no direct connection to municipal government. School boards in these districts are responsible for setting policy, approving budgets, and making decisions on local revenue. Dependent districts generally have policymaking authority, but rely on cities and towns and their governance structures to determine the amount of local funding for the school districts.

Governance of Charter and Pilot Schools

The governance structure in charter schools varies depending on state policy. Legislation in some states requires the State Board of Education to review charter school proposals and approve or reject them. The proposals must include the governance structure the charter school will use, typically a governing board that includes members of the group that formulated the proposal, such as educators and community members. The only role of the local school district where the state issues the charter is to provide funding for the students who attend the charter school. Another approach available in some states permits local school boards to approve "in-district" charter schools that have their own governing boards and autonomy similar to that granted to state-approved charter schools. With this model, the local school district has some oversight responsibility and is expected to intervene if the schools are not meeting the goals incorporated in the charter agreement.

Pilot schools are similar in design to in-district charter schools. The innovative school model was generated during contract negotiations between the Boston Teachers Union and the Boston Public Schools (BPS) in 1994, when the first charter schools were opening in Boston and some students were beginning to leave BPS to attend them. The Massachusetts policy required the State Board of Education to approve charter school proposals and assigned responsibility for their oversight to the Massachusetts Department of Education. Some states took a similar approach, and others created policies that gave local school boards the authority to approve proposals for charter schools that would open in their school districts as in-district charter schools. Policy in some states allowed for both the independent charter school model with the charter issued by the state as well as the in-district model that required approval by the school board.

The partnership between the Boston Teachers Union and BPS was a breakthrough in collaboration between labor and management.

A new Joint Labor Management Committee, cochaired by the union president and the superintendent, was responsible for reviewing all proposals submitted by those seeking permission to create new pilot schools, and for voting to approve or deny the proposals. The process for approving or denying pilot school proposals is contained in the collective bargaining contract and reflects the governance structures of both the union and the school committee. The superintendent selects five school and district leaders, and the union president selects five teachers and other union leaders to serve on the committee. The superintendent and union president each have veto power to override a vote of the committee. (The veto was not a factor until a new union president held up approval of additional pilot school proposals during contract negotiations in 2005.) By 2010, there were twenty-two pilot schools representing the full range of both new start-up and conversion schools with differentiated grade-level configurations. Proposals for start-up schools can be developed by ad hoc groups who convene to do so. In addition to start-up schools, current schools may develop and submit proposals to convert to pilot school status. A vote of two-thirds or more of the faculty is required to develop and approve a school conversion proposal and submit it to the Joint Labor Management Committee and the school committee for approval.

What is the difference between charter and pilot schools? In charter schools, the governing board hires the principal. Pilot school governing boards have hiring authority as well, but the superintendent does have veto authority, which has rarely been exercised in BPS. Pilot schools have the autonomy to hire staff, but if there is a district layoff of teachers, the pilot school teachers are not exempt. Once hired, pilot school teachers cannot be paid less than what the union-negotiated salary schedule requires. The governing boards in the pilot schools have flexibility to establish the work agreement that covers the length of the work day and work year for staff, and other conditions of employment. Moreover, a pilot school teacher is guaranteed a teaching assignment in a regular Boston public school if he or she decides to leave the pilot school for reasons other than poor performance.

Cogovernance Structures

One of the greatest challenges for superintendents, school boards, principals, and charter or pilot school boards is to have the difficult conversations about the roles and responsibilities of each and the shared accountability that is necessary for each to succeed and for goals to be achieved. The board chair has a challenging role. The chair's leadership skills are essential in building board effectiveness. The board's most important role is to hire and evaluate the superintendent in a school district or a school leader for a charter school; set annual goals for the board, superintendent, or charter school leader to reach; take fiduciary responsibility for district or school budgets and finances; consider and act on policies and other matters recommended by the superintendent, school leaders, or staff; and avoid micromanagement of the superintendents or school leaders who are responsible and accountable for leading and managing school districts and schools.

Boards that micromanage their leaders eventually will lose them. And sometimes boards hire leaders who want job security and will do whatever their boards tell them to do to ensure it, even when it may not be in the best interest of all students or of the teachers, principals, and other staff who have the responsibility to educate them. There is also a danger when a board functions as a rubber stamp for the superintendent or school leader and loses credibility with its constituencies for approving most or all of the recommendations that the superintendent or school leader presents. This is why the time spent during the hiring process is so important for school boards and district and school leaders. Clarifying expectations, goals, rules of engagement, and accountability, and determining how the boards, superintendents, and school leaders will build positive relationships and develop partnerships, are essential at the outset when a new superintendent of a school district or leader of a charter or other type of school that has its own governing board is appointed. Periodic facilitated retreats scheduled for boards and district or school leaders to continue to discuss working relationships, establish goals, and determine expectations for performance can be very helpful in establishing a culture of partnership, collaboration, and continuous learning, which are characteristics notable in high-performing school districts and schools.

In many states, there are requirements for all public schools to have some kind of governance structure that requires school leaders to work with a school site council, the PTA, or other community groups. School site councils usually are structured so as to ensure the participation of parents, teachers, principals, and perhaps other staff. In secondary schools, student representatives often are members of the governance group. Parents elect parent representatives, teachers elect their colleagues, and the student council or a similar student group elects the student representatives. The council may elect its chair, or there may be a rotation practice that provides opportunities for the principal, a teacher, a staff member, or a parent to serve in that role.

In some schools, cochairs share leadership roles. The responsibilities vary, but usually involve review of the school improvement plan, the school budget, and other issues of interest to the members. Formal action by vote is required in some districts. Superintendents often ask staff and parent and community representatives to serve on selection committees when principal candidates are being considered. Principals will encounter challenges in working with school-based groups that are similar in some ways to what district leaders experience in working with school boards. The stakes are not as high, but the leadership skills required to engage and help people reach consensus on how to support the school and its mission to serve every child are important.

Both the chair of the school site council and the principal have leadership roles. The chair should be helping other members of the council understand their roles and responsibilities and engage them in developing the protocols they will follow to create a collaborative working relationship with the principal and staff. The relationship between a principal and a charter or pilot school board also should be built on mutual respect, clear understanding of roles and responsibilities, shared vision for the school, effective communication and transparency, shared accountability for results, and the commitment to determine what data must be gathered to inform the discussion about how the jointly developed targets for success are or are not being reached.

The Principal's Role Expanded

Prior to the 1990s, most principals were trained to be good managers who knew how to deal with the many operational tasks that all schools must manage. With the advent of standards-based reform, the role of the principal expanded. With the quality of instruction in classrooms clearly the most important variable the schools could address to improve student achievement, principals were required to focus on teaching and learning and become instructional leaders. Responsibility for operations did not end; but to succeed as an instructional leader, the principal had to learn how to avoid becoming bogged down with operations and focus on selecting the best people to staff the school, understand the leader's responsibility for building the capacity of the teachers and other staff to be continuous learners and to perform at high levels, and engage the staff in the development of an accountability system that includes measures to determine student growth and continuous improvement.

Relationship building is the most important skill for the leaders of school boards, districts, and schools. Communication skills based on "no surprises" and transparency are essential as well.

Relationship building is the most important skill for the leaders of school boards, districts, and schools.

Leaders at all levels in a school district must have a keen sense of what information to share with others and when and how to share it. Timely access to information is essential for leaders and followers to perform at high levels. Transparency is an essential ingredient in building trust and supporting a culture of collaboration in school districts and schools. Leaders want the best information available to make appropriate and timely decisions. Random, untimely surprises can negate effective decision making. Collaboration in developing budgets to align with district and school education plans is essential to ensure that districts and schools will bring coherence to their work to improve teaching and learning for all students and generate the results promised to the students and families they serve.

Resource Allocation

Writing now in 2010, I can reflect on the periodic cycles of opportunities I had to add much-needed resources to district and school budgets during good times, and conversely the challenging necessities to make deep budget cuts during bad times. However, the budget challenges facing school districts across the country in 2010 and probably looking ahead to 2011 and beyond are more daunting than any I have experienced in the last forty years. As an executive coach for several first-time superintendents in large urban school districts, I found that the following was the typical scenario in 2010:

In many urban districts, enrollment is declining. The major sources of funding, state revenue and local property taxes, are shrinking. Eighty to eighty-five percent of the district budget covers salaries and benefits for district employees, most of whom are teachers. The goal is to keep cuts from affecting the classrooms in schools. The superintendent has proposed some central office cuts, but the savings will be modest and not significant in closing the gap between proposed expenditures and available revenue. The parents are lobbying to keep cuts away from the schools and do not want the arts, music, and physical education teachers cut at the elementary schools. The union supports the teachers, who are adamant that the class size reductions of several years ago be maintained and that jobs not be cut. The teachers union refuses to reopen the contract and consider ways to save money. The school board is unable to reach consensus on how to make the cuts. It requires the superintendent to make recommendations. The superintendent suggests that each school's principal and school site council should decide how to make the cuts. The board agrees, and the leadership challenge is handed off to the principals, who have been asking for more autonomy in making decisions about budget priorities. How will the principals address this leadership challenge and seek consensus among the staff and parents to make a decision that is focused on the interests of the children—which may be different from the interests of at least some of the adults?

There can be no resolution without facing the reality that 80 percent or more of the budget is allocated for salaries and benefits and that to balance the budget there must be significant reductions in the number of positions allocated to the schools.

The Art of Politics

Educators often eschew politics, but leaders in education do so at their peril. District and school leaders need not fear politics. They are wise to have ethical standards that guide their engagement in politics, and to remember, as Bismarck said in the nineteenth century, that "politics is the art of the possible."

> *Educators often eschew politics, but leaders in education do so at their peril.*

District Level—Compromise, Common Sense, and Consistency

At the district level, superintendents report to boards, which vote on their recommendations. Certainly superintendents want their boards to endorse what they as educators recommend, but legitimate differences of opinion will surface, particularly with controversial issues—for example, decisions about resource allocation, school consolidations, selection of curricula, personnel appointments, attendance boundaries, collective bargaining contracts, and community issues that may seem unrelated to the public schools but somehow find their way to the schoolhouse doors. Unanimous school board votes to support the superintendent's recommendations are what superintendents strive to achieve, but if they appear over time to be swift and automatic, a restless public may begin to view their elected school board as a rubber stamp for the superintendent, which can erode the influence of the district leader as the primary advocate for children and the top educator in the community.

Split boards where members vote in blocks and rarely reach consensus are a challenge for any leader. The core values of all parties are tested in such settings, and the district and school leaders must determine where there is room for compromise. Certainly leaders must be willing to compromise, remembering that the goal is to reach a middle ground rather than fold one's flag and retreat. However, it is wise for leaders to think about what situations they might face that could result in such egregious attacks on their core values that they would have to step down and leave their positions rather than compromise their integrity. Kenny Rogers's song "The Gambler" is a good reference point for successful leaders: "You got to know when to hold 'em, know when to fold 'em, know when to walk away, and know when to run."

> *Kenny Rogers's song "The Gambler" is a good reference point for successful leaders.*

Leaders do need to know well the members of their governance boards. They may not agree with the positions that some board members take or the votes they cast, but they should treat all members with respect. Communications protocols must be clear, transparent, and consistently followed. It is fine for district leaders to meet individually with their board members and for school leaders to meet with their site council or governing board members individually, but I have found that the practice of district and school leaders giving the same information to all board members is best. It is difficult to give equal time to each board member. It is necessary for the chair of the board and superintendent to spend time together to plan meeting agendas, confer about the work of the board, and discuss the political challenges they face. Leaders who share information with some board members and not others are likely to foster an atmosphere of distrust among them, which can result in dysfunction. Transparency in my experience is essential.

School Level—Instructional Leadership Teams (ILTs)

The dynamics are similar for school leaders, although the issues may be more narrowly focused on the individual school's needs and interests. The principal must understand the internal politics within the school as well as among the parents and community groups in the area served by the school. Outreach is important. Sincerity and transparency also are critical. It is easy to aspire to a culture of collaboration in the school, but such a culture is difficult to achieve against the power of the traditional structure of schools, with teachers spending most of their day isolated in classrooms, working with their students without the benefits of engaging with their colleagues in team efforts and focusing on learning from each other how to improve their instruction and the performance of all students in the school.

The principal has a great opportunity to create an ILT that can be responsible for working collaboratively to develop the school's improvement plan based on the shared goal of having a laser-like focus on instructional improvement in every classroom. The principal chooses teacher-leaders who are respected by their colleagues for the quality of their instruction and for their knowledge of curriculum, commitment to collaborative learning, skills in analyzing data, and willingness to help design the school plan and participate in the preparation of the school's budget to ensure that it becomes the financial plan that aligns resources to support the execution of the education plan. The ILT members help the principal seek advice from colleagues and generate the support for the development and implementation of the plan. The work of the ILT validates the principal's commitment to shared leadership and the importance of building a school culture that supports a professional learning community.

By sharing leadership, the principal models the behavior necessary to move the school from a culture of isolation to a culture of collaboration.

Student Leadership—An Undervalued Resource

District and school leaders must provide students with leadership opportunities. Creating opportunities for students to learn about and engage in politics through experiences in schools provides early lessons for civic responsibility in a democracy and opportunities to participate in ways that will serve the common good. It is not too early to start in elementary schools, where students can run for leadership positions in their classrooms and schools. By middle school, students are eager to design their own campaigns for leadership positions and experience how politics and governance work. Opportunities for leadership expand significantly in high school through sports, school publications, debate teams, science fairs, service clubs, class offices, bands, orchestras, theater, student councils, and many other areas. Another way is to include students in the various governance structures that exist in schools and school districts. School boards may have a student member who is elected by a districtwide student advisory council of representatives from each high school and serves in an ex-officio capacity with the opportunity to participate in conversations about policies at board meetings but not cast a vote.

For example, the Boston Student Advisory Council (BSAC) elects a student to serve as an ex-officio member of the school committee. The superintendent meets periodically with the council to discuss policy issues and to engage students to help shape them. One year, at the request of the superintendent, BSAC was asked to work on the controversial issue of student use of cell phones during the school day. The group spent several months talking with students, principals, parents, and others and developing a proposed policy for consideration by the superintendent and school committee. The students made presentations at the school committee meetings, and their final policy proposal was adopted. The credibility of the policy, despite differences of opinion that surfaced during the debate about its final form, was significantly enhanced because of the important role students played in its development and the implementation of the policy in the schools. They learned about the internal politics in schools and the external politics they encountered in the community and with special interest groups, and used their new knowledge to achieve a unanimous vote approving a cell phone policy that included key provisions they recommended.

Student roles such as those mentioned here are available at all school levels. Students in the upper elementary grades greatly benefit from involvement in school site councils, and at the secondary school level, there are opportunities to serve on a council or similar governance body. In some school districts, high school screening committees that include student representatives are convened to interview candidates for the principal position. Students who have opportunities to gain experience with governance have an important perspective to share and may be motivated to aspire to leadership positions in schools and school districts in the future. Effective district and school leaders understand that student voice is an important asset. Moreover, students must gain experience by participating in the political arena and learning the importance of citizens' roles in keeping democracy vibrant and effective.

Student Researchers

The Boston Plan for Excellence (BPE), a public education fund and supporter of the systemic reform work in BPS, provided financial support for external evaluations of several aspects of the district's reform work. With the backing of BPS, the BPE decided to offer high school students who were interested in educational research the opportunity to spend a year in an after-school pro gram learning how to become educational researchers and create a research project that they would use to gather data in a sample of Boston's high schools. They designed a study of school climate that would be based on data gathered from samples of students in thirteen high schools. They designed and conducted the survey, analyzed the data, wrote individual reports with analyses for each of the thirteen schools, and prepared a comprehensive summary document that included the aggregate analyses of the data from all the schools. Initially the results were shared with each of the high school principals and the superintendent.

The findings were compelling and controversial because they revealed the students' views about student-to-student, adult-to-adult, and student-to-adult relationships—with the conclusion that significant improvement was needed to improve the relationships among the people in the schools and the climate for teaching and learning. Some school leaders and faculty challenged the results and denied their accuracy; others accepted them and began the difficult conversations about how to improve school climate. In my role as superintendent, I invited several of the student researchers to present the report to the school committee at a public meeting. In my back-to-school message at the beginning of the next school year, I challenged adults in the school system to lead by example and take responsibility for improving relationships in the schools as an important part of the work to improve the quality of instruction and the climate for teaching and learning throughout the district.

Student engagement in serious work outside the classroom walls, although it could potentially disturb the status quo and create some political unrest, often results in positive outcomes. The students who began their work learning how to conduct high-quality research, develop survey documents, create a sample of students to complete surveys, analyze data, draw conclusions, make recommendations, and write and present their report confronted political challenges when the report was released. It brought the discussion about school climate and relationships among those in schools into the public square for discussion.

Some principals embraced the data analysis and findings in the report. Others were not eager to make their individual school reports public. The participating students learned a great deal about politics and the challenge of going public with results that were accepted by some and rejected by others, where the credibility of the work was praised by some and ignored by others, and gained the experience of presenting their findings at a public meeting of the Boston School Committee, which generated news coverage and recognition of their impressive work.

Policies

District and school leaders do not have the luxury of compartmentalizing important components of leadership. Each has its unique features, often shaped by context. Sometimes leaders must seize the moment and push for change quickly, before opponents can muster counterforces to block. And there are times when leaders must proceed more slowly and deliberatively to develop support and build not only the capacity to create a change and improvement plan but also the capacity of the people who will be assigned to implement it.

When governance, politics, and policies align, they can be powerful allies for district and school leaders whose job it is to focus on the improvement of teaching and learning in every classroom and for all children. However, district and school leaders usually encounter mixed messages from federal, state, and local education policymakers. Policies can be difficult to navigate because they are established at several levels and by both the legislative and executive branches of government, and are also often interpreted by the court system.

How should a leader counter potential political battles and successfully interpret and implement policy? Timing is critical, and cultivation of support at the time that policy is formulated and presented to the school board for approval is essential. Certainly leaders who provide opportunities for both proponents and opponents to review proposed policies before they are recommended for school board consideration and approval will have information that may help determine how to modify and improve the proposed policy in anticipation of the challenges that may be forthcoming from opponents. It is important for leaders to know where they are willing to compromise and make modifications and what is essential to retain and not subject to compromise.

The Policy Pyramid

In America, state legislatures, state boards of education, and local school boards have major responsibility for making public education policy. The federal government's role has been limited but significant, particularly when there has been a national interest important enough to justify federal policy rather than policies created by fifty different states. Examples of significant federal policy in recent decades would include civil rights legislation of the 1960s, the Elementary and Secondary Education Act, the Individuals with Disabilities Education Act, and the

No Child Left Behind Act. Many of the policies in these bills as well as decisions in state and federal court cases have addressed equity issues and affected policies for funding school districts and schools, with the requirement that the regulations interpreting the intent of the legislation and court decisions would be followed as a condition for receiving federal or state funds.

The U.S. Department of Education is responsible for developing the federal rules and regulations for the education legislation passed by Congress and signed by the president. The regulations provide guidance for states, school districts, and schools that qualify for the federal programs and the money Congress appropriates to fund them. State departments of education are responsible for determining that the funds are allocated to qualifying school districts and that they are spent in ways intended by federal policy. A similar process is followed at the state level, where policies are passed by state legislatures and signed by governors and boards of education, and state departments of education function as administrative agencies responsible for ensuring that local school districts and schools implement the policies. The intent has been to hold school boards and the leaders of school districts and schools accountable for implementing the federal and state policies with fidelity. The expectation is that the school districts and schools will comply with federal and state regulations for implementing the federal and state policy. All too often the compliance measures and the checklists that record them do not align well with the intent of the policies, which also require qualitative assessments to understand what is and is not working.

The third level of education policymaking is the local school board. District and school leaders should be active in helping shape policy as well as in accepting responsibility for implementing it. The president often proposes legislation for Congress to enact. Governors do the same with state legislatures and sometimes with their state boards of education. District leaders have a similar role with school boards and, when appropriate, must consult with school leaders on the effectiveness of existing policies and on proposals for new ones. Once school boards adopt policy, the superintendent, in consultation with other district and school leaders, has the responsibility for establishing administrative rules and regulations to guide the implementation of policy. However, district and school leaders have dual responsibility because they also are accountable for the implementation of policy and the results achieved.

Compliance Challenges

The multiple sources of policies and the lack of alignment and coherence often evident among them create challenges for district and school leaders who are responsible for making the policies work and generating positive results. Usually the means for determining whether leaders are doing what they are expected to do is to focus on what it means to comply. Leaders have to avoid the cynicism that a narrow definition of compliance may create. Compliance documents usually are designed to empower those who bear the responsibility for ensuring that the rules and regulations for carrying out policy are closely followed. An unintended consequence occurs when the standards for compliance focus more on process than on outcomes, causing leaders to spend inordinate amounts of time documenting how they followed the rules, with few expectations for producing evidence of student performance outcomes. Over the many years of my own leadership experience, I have often faced external review teams entering the districts and schools I have led and judging me and my colleagues based solely on whether we have—or have not—followed procedures. This is not to say that accountability for processes and procedures is unreasonable, provided that it enables leaders to better understand the connections between processes and procedures and the impact they will have on strategies for improving teaching and learning. Context is also an important variable, one that often cannot be captured by the one-size-fits-all compliance checklist.

With the No Child Left Behind (NCLB) legislation, the focus has shifted to student achievement, with all students expected to reach proficiency standards by a fixed date: 2014. The legislation has been controversial, with supporters and adversaries arguing over both the policy focus and the mechanics of implementation. Each of the fifty states sets its own standards for what students should know and be able to do, creates its own assessments aligned with its standards to measure student progress, establishes the requirements for meeting achievement targets on the state tests, and reports the outcomes annually. The one assessment the federal government uses to compare student achievement among the states is the National Assessment of Educational Progress (NAEP). These results show wide variations among the states. The gaps between student performance at the proficiency level on the NAEP and on state assessments are significant, proving that there is wide variation in the rigor of the state assessments in relation to the standard for proficiency on the NAEP.

The goal of NCLB is for all students to reach proficiency by 2014, but there are fifty different standards of proficiency. This creates a good deal of ambiguity for district and school leaders, as well as consternation with the metric created for accountability purposes. However, the requirement that assessment results be disaggregated by race, income, disability, and first language has been an important breakthrough for shining the light on populations of students who have not received the support they need to succeed because their data were masked by the practice of reporting only aggregate scores for all students. Increasing numbers of school districts and schools are not meeting the annual targets for improvement based on the NCLB metric, which defines adequate yearly progress (AYP), a label that schools receive even if they miss student achievement targets in only one or two categories among dozens.

Although the AYP metric does not reflect fairly the degree to which school districts and schools succeed in progressing toward the goals established by the policy of getting all students to proficiency, the requirement to disaggregate student data has been essential to reveal the gaps that exist. These data underscore the imperative duty for district and school leaders to close the achievement gaps and ensure that all students achieve the same high standards that in the past only select groups of children had been expected to reach. Of course the pressure on leaders is great—but the policy direction shaped by standards-based reform is necessary to accomplish the goal. Now that it is much clearer what leaders need to do with the shifts in policy, the current focus for leaders is to take instructional improvement in school districts and schools to scale. The compliance framework used in the past to measure whether policies were implemented will not succeed in yielding the achievement outcomes driven by standards. Leaders know what needs to be done, but significant support is still necessary to help leaders learn how to improve instruction in all districts, schools, and classrooms.

Quality, Not Just Quantity

NCLB established the expectations for the types of assessments states must use for accountability purposes. The assessments must generate quantitative data that determine the status of school districts and schools, using their progress in meeting achievement targets to ascertain whether AYP is reached. Prior to NCLB, some states had their own accountability systems, and they may still use both the state and federal accountability systems for reporting data. Often there is weak alignment between the two, creating great confusion among educators, parents, and community members when they are confronted with varying sets of data that often lead to different conclusions. The incompatibility of the two systems must be addressed and resolved. Early in 2010, President Obama and Secretary of Education Duncan announced that the reauthorization of the Elementary and Secondary Education Act—intended in part to address the shortcomings of NCLB—would be a priority of the administration, and would, they hoped, be completed before the end of the year. This is a necessary and ambitious goal, but it may be difficult to accomplish before the end of 2010.

The results of assessments used for accountability purposes do not sufficiently support any comprehensive judgments about what is and is not working in our schools and classrooms. Qualitative assessments are also necessary to judge the quality of instruction and fidelity of implementation of curriculum and programs in classrooms. This requires instruments that focus on the characteristics observable in high-performing schools and classrooms. What are the elements of effective teaching in classrooms and of effective leadership in schools? As more evidence emerges about best practices—on such topics as curriculum and pedagogy, teaching, and alignment among standards, curriculum, and assessment—we will have better ways to use qualitative as well as quantitative test data to determine the effectiveness of both teaching and learning.

Budgeting for Achievement and Equity

The realities of funding and the challenges district and school leaders face in tapping federal, state, and local public funds as well as foundation and other sources for financial resources require both technical and political skills that can be learned. In my experience, I cannot remember a budget that in any year enabled me to do everything that I knew was necessary to give all children the opportunity to learn. We want children to reach the same level of learning and achievement, but because of their differentiated needs, an equal per-pupil expenditure is not sufficient to meet this goal.

District and school leaders must play two roles during the annual budget process. First, leaders must be strong advocates and make the case for resources to do what they explicitly believe will enable all the children in their district or school to achieve no less than a year's growth in achievement. In urban districts and schools where too many children have fallen behind, the goals must be more ambitious and require accelerated growth to reduce the gaps and enhance the opportunities for those who are behind to catch up and succeed. It takes courage and political will to ask for more resources for some students when the norm is to demonstrate fairness by giving the same amount to most if not all students. Equity is the value leaders must embrace as advocates for all the children they serve. This means more resources will be needed for English language learners, students with disabilities, low-income students, gifted students, and any others who may have fallen behind. When school boards are making decisions on how to allocate resources in the annual budget, I have often seen that the children who need advocates the most are the ones least likely to have organized advocacy from the community.

The second role that leaders must fill begins the minute the final decisions on budget are made by the decision makers. Successful school district and school leaders then become advocates for doing the best they, and those they lead, can with the available resources—eliminating the excuse of inadequate funding. In short, successful leaders will not tolerate those who whine and make excuses for failure to improve teaching and learning by blaming inadequate resources. They will enable their followers to use existing resources wisely, based on the priorities they have set for improving student achievement.

> *Successful school district and school leaders become advocates for doing the best they, and those they lead, can with the available resources.*

Leaders must hold themselves and those they lead accountable for expecting growth in learning, a minimum of a year of growth in student achievement for a year of school, and accelerated progress where achievement gaps must be closed. Moreover, leaders must continue to look for other sources of funding from district and school partners, local business and community organization foundations, and other grant opportunities. There will be times when school district and school leaders must determine how to take their case for additional resources to the taxpayers and use the political process to convince local taxpayers to override a cap for raising tax revenue to support the education of the community's children, or join others in backing candidates who will shape education policy at the state and federal levels.

Collective Bargaining, Contracts, and Compensation

A chapter on the impact governance, politics, and policies have on school district and school leadership would be incomplete without attention to the impact that public employee collective bargaining has had since the early 1960s, when some states began to legislate policies that gave teacher associations and unions and other public employees the right to bargain with school boards for contracts that determined wages, hours, and terms and conditions of employment. The first states to pass public employee collective bargaining policies were states with strong union presence in other sectors and where collective bargaining already was the norm. Right-to-work states at the outset were not interested in changing their workforce policies and still do not have policies requiring public employee collective bargaining.

The American Federation of Teachers (AFT) took the lead in the 1960s when Albert Shanker, the leader of the New York City teachers union, negotiated the first major public school district teachers union contract and used a strike as a significant lever to reach agreement on key union demands. And the success that he had in bargaining the contract in the nation's largest urban school district became the reference point for expanding the influence of the AFT, primarily in states that already had private sector collective bargaining. The National Education Association (NEA), the largest national organization of teachers and the major competitor with the AFT, continued to market the organization as a professional association that would not engage in collective bargaining because it was not appropriate for professionals to do so. The NEA did change its position as more states began to pass public employee collective bargaining legislation in the late 1960s and early 1970s.

Throughout my career as a superintendent, I have worked in five states (Pennsylvania, Oregon, Oklahoma, California, and Massachusetts) with public employee collective bargaining statutes. The irony was that in 1967, I wrote my qualifying paper, which was required by the doctoral program at the Harvard Graduate School of Education as the last hurdle before choosing a dissertation topic, on the politics of passing the public employee collective bargaining legislation in Massachusetts. In 1967, I had no premonition about the impact collective bargaining would have on the allocation of my time and the demands for the improvement of leadership skills during the next forty years. During my career, I experienced two strikes and several other close calls when strike votes had been approved by the union, only to be averted by settlement agreements reached at the eleventh hour.

Although teachers were the initial focus of public employee collective bargaining in school districts, other district employees began to join unions as well. The employees who did not work in positions requiring state certification were represented by classified employee unions. In some states, principals and designated central office management employees are unionized and have the right to collective bargaining. My fifth and final position as superintendent was in BPS. When I arrived in 1995, more than twenty-five years after the passage of public employee collective bargaining legislation in Massachusetts, there were thirty-two different bargaining units representing employees of the City of Boston, which included BPS. Two years before I arrived, the state legislature had agreed to remove principals from collective bargaining and provided superintendents with the authority to appoint principals to serve on one-, two-, or three-year contracts. Although principals were no longer represented by a union, thirteen of the thirty-two bargaining units in the city were in BPS, and the largest in the city was the teachers union affiliated with the AFT.

The Roles of the Superintendent and School Board

The size of the district will define in part the superintendent's role in collective bargaining. In small districts, the superintendent may be at the bargaining table taking the lead for the district in the negotiations with the bargaining units. In larger districts, there is a separate office that focuses on the development of the district's proposals; works with the district's bargaining team, which may include several leaders from the central office and perhaps one or two principals from the schools; and joins the superintendent in discussions with the school board in executive sessions to determine the priorities the district will present in its proposals and what the responses will be to the union's proposals. Communication between the superintendent, the district bargaining team, and the school board is essential. Confidentiality also is essential and cannot be breached. The superintendent and board chair must be clear that it is inappropriate for them to talk with constituents about contract proposals during negotiations. In some districts, a member of the board may be on the district's negotiation team. I do not favor that approach because it puts too much pressure on a single board member when it is necessary to bring the total board together on collective bargaining strategies and fidelity of execution and message. While at the bargaining table, there should be one member of the team assigned the role of spokesperson who will speak for the team and decide when to have other members of the team engage in the conversation. On both sides of the bargaining table, each team member is listening to determine whether a signal from the other side has been inadvertently sent that may strengthen or weaken the opponent's position, which may redirect strategies on both sides of the table.

States with right-to-work statutes do not provide collective bargaining rights for public employees. In these states, district and school leaders may be members of associations that have informal conversations with superintendents or school boards about contracts and compensation. However, the practices are not uniform from state to state or between school districts within a state. The way in which contracts and compensation are decided is greatly influenced by context. Most states have policies determining how teachers and other public school district and school employees do or do not obtain tenure. Superintendents, with the exception of one or two states, are not granted tenure in position. State statutes vary on tenure rights for teachers, principals, and other classifications of school district and school employees. Policies also vary on how decisions on contracts and compensation are made.

In right-to-work states public employee collective bargaining is not required. A few right-to-work states do establish a teacher salary schedule that school districts are required to follow. There are a few examples of school districts in right-to-work states that have decided locally to engage in conversations with the local teacher organizations about working conditions, salaries, and benefits. However, this is not required, and the local school board must agree to this approach. Local school boards are involved in approving contracts and establishing compensation policy, even though the policy on how to do so varies from state to state, as already noted.

In the places that require collective bargaining, the school board or its representatives must negotiate with the unions or organizations representing employee groups and also approve the resulting contract. The collective bargaining contract usually covers wages, hours, and other terms and conditions of employment for the employees in the bargaining unit covered by the contract. The basic issues addressed include the number of days in the school year, length of the work day, the time for required professional development, planning time for teachers during the school day, and maximum class sizes. However, in some states the scope of bargaining has been expanded to include work rules and other issues that were traditionally part of management's prerogatives. In states where collective bargaining does not exist, informal meet-and-confer arrangements exist between representatives of employee organizations and school districts, but the outcome of the informal deliberations is usually not binding, and the school board makes the final decisions on salaries and benefits.

In the private sector, generally there is a clearer delineation between management and labor than exists in the public sector. In some collective bargaining states, all public school district and school employees except the superintendent and a senior management group are members of collective bargaining units. When this isn't the case, the superintendent normally has the responsibility for working with the school board to determine policies governing the hiring of personnel, the issuing of contracts, and the establishment of compensation plans. The superintendent's contract typically results from consultation between the board and superintendent at the time of hiring. It is not unusual for the board to have its attorney negotiate the contract with an attorney hired by the superintendent. Contracts have become more and more complex in recent years, with the addition of great detail on expectations each party has for the other and of incentive plans with compensation tied to student performance results. Superintendents' contract lengths tend to be three to four years, but some have provisions for a one-year rollover after the annual evaluation. As mentioned earlier, in urban school districts, the turnover of superintendents is quite high, with the average tenure lasting three years or less. My view is that the most important governance decision a school board makes is the selection of a superintendent—and the most important decisions that district and school leaders make are personnel decisions, because effective leadership at the district and school levels is essential and second only to the quality of instruction in the classroom in affecting student achievement.

Despite my extensive experience with collective bargaining, continuous learning was essential. I have seen a dramatic broadening of the scope of negotiations in many states and school districts, with the result that many contracts now have several hundred pages of work rules that can block needed innovation and changes in the practice of leadership in school districts and schools. However, I believe that all positions in public school districts and schools held by those with management and supervision responsibilities should be excluded from collective bargaining. Personnel in these categories should either have fixed-term contracts or serve at the will of the superintendent.

In states where the school board has responsibility for approving all personnel appointments, the superintendent presents the personnel recommendations for school board approval. Ultimately the superintendent is held accountable for selection of personnel and for their performance. School board members should not pressure the superintendent to select particular candidates—because if the candidate is not the right fit and fails to perform, it's the superintendent, not the school board, who will have to correct the situation.

State policy can make a positive difference by addressing the roles of superintendents and principals through legislation. Massachusetts serves as a good example. In 1993, the legislature in the Commonwealth of Massachusetts passed a broad education reform bill with a provision that gave superintendents control over personnel decisions; removed school principals from collective bargaining; and made principals eligible for one-, two-, or three-year contracts determined by the district superintendent. This provided superintendents with great flexibility in making personnel decisions, with very clear expectations about the accountability for results. However, other certified administrators, such as assistant principals and middle-level central office administrators, are still entitled to collective bargaining rights and may be represented by employee unions or organizations. Classified managerial employees and senior-level certificated administrators also are exempt from collective bargaining in Massachusetts.

In recent years I have seen changes in compensation plans for educators, and I expect they will continue to evolve. The salaries and benefits for superintendents serving in urban and many afflu-ent suburban communities have increased significantly in the early years of the twenty-first century. Many contracts for superinten-dents now include opportunities for annual bonuses in addition to whatever base salary increases are guaranteed by contract. Bonuses are based on reaching specific student achievement gains, narrowing achievement gaps, and meeting other specified targets, such as teacher recruitment, hiring and retention rates, and bal-anced budgets. Community relations and relationships with the district employees and the school board are not easy to measure with quantitative metrics. However, they can be assessed with qualitative indicators that describe the behavior of leaders.

Supply and demand also are factors in crafting compensa-tion plans as larger numbers of teachers and administrators reach retirement age and senior-level leaders in central office posi-tions are reluctant to take on the top-level positions. Whereas three-year contracts for superintendents have been the norm in most urban school districts, contracts of four and five years now are being used by more school boards as incentives to attract and retain the best candidates. Reducing turnover by retaining suc-cessful superintendents and providing them with the opportunity to have a positive impact is essential to improve a whole system of schools rather than leaving a legacy of only a few more good ones.

Compensation plans for some other school and central office leaders are defined by collective bargaining contracts in states with public employee collective bargaining for administrators. Negotiations with these bargaining units are similar to those with teachers and other employee groups, but tend to focus on salaries and benefits and not work rules. Salary schedules recommended by the superintendent and approved by the school board are the norm in many places. In large districts, there may be a small group of leaders at the deputy or assistant superintendent levels whose salaries are based on the evaluation by the superintendent and in some cases on performance goals, including student achievement.

The range of compensation plans for school leaders is similar. However, the trend seems to be moving in the direction of including annual performance indicators and an assessment of the district or school leader's success in reaching them as significant factors in determining compensation. Meanwhile, policy debates on how to link teacher compensation to student achievement are increasing, with strong resistance from the teachers unions and cautionary tales from some researchers who question the validity and reliability of the results of some assessments being used for this purpose. We are likely to see this issue persist at the nexus of governance, politics, and policies with the reauthorization of the Elementary and Secondary Education Act.

President Obama and the secretary of education, Arne Duncan, have set expectations for those applying for federal education funds, such as Race to the Top, innovation, school improvement, and Turnaround School grants, which must be used for innovation, change, and improvement in states, school districts, and schools. Among the most controversial requirements that states and school districts must submit with their grant applications is evidence, including union sign-off supporting the commitment to performance management plans that will use student achievement data as an important outcome measure, to determine the effectiveness of the proposals. Local teachers union sign-off on the proposals has created resistance to the grants in some states and school districts. However, the president of the AFT has said that there may be ways to consider some type of performance pay for teachers, depending on how it is designed. As of early spring 2010, the NEA has not expressed interest in performance management or performance pay for teachers that would use student achievement results as a major measure.

One example from my own experience illustrates how difficult it is to implement an innovative approach to compensation. During my first year as superintendent in Boston, I was able to set aside a modest amount of money in the budget to provide a bonus for the most successful principals. However, the suburban districts were raising the base pay for their principals, and to stay competitive and stem the exodus of Boston principals to the suburbs, I had to use the bonus money to raise the base for all principals in Boston. This was the challenge for me every year. I was never able to maintain a separate bonus fund because base salaries were going up faster than the number of dollars available to support bonuses and stay competitive with other districts.

Moreover, in many cases superintendents volunteer (or submit to a request from the school board) not to take an increase that may be guaranteed in their contracts. And sometimes school boards refuse to grant a bonus even when performance measures are met or exceeded, because a collective bargaining agreement with one or more unions has not been reached or because revenue shortfalls require major budget cuts. These realities work against the push for performance-based pay because the level of performance may not align with the vicissitudes of budget cycles, the amount of revenue available to honor the bonus, and the politics of providing a superintendent or principal with a bonus when other employees receive more modest salary increases. These are some of the challenges for leaders as they consider performance pay and search for ways to make it credible: developing transparent indicators that will determine how performance is awarded and figuring out how to honor the commitment to performance improvement when budget resources to finance other district priorities are scarce.

Public education governance structures in America have not changed much in recent decades. Most local school boards are elected by the public. As noted earlier, during the last decade some large cities have begun having school boards appointed by the mayor. At the state level, there have been some changes in the mix of appointed and elected state boards of education. Although still limited, the role of the federal government in setting policy and providing funding has increased since the 1960s. However, federal dollars have provided only 6 to 8 percent of the money spent annually on elementary and secondary education in America.

During my career as an educator, I have observed dramatic changes in politics. The national political conventions demonstrate the shift. In 1952, for the first time, the Republicans and Democrats both held televised national conventions. I was not quite twelve that summer and spent as much time as possible at my grandparents' house where there was a newly purchased black-and-white television. I became fascinated with the medium and followed the process of each convention. It was agonizing to try to understand all the debate and wrangling about the "platform." The exciting part would be the nomination of the party's candidate for president, which did not occur until the final day of the convention. Finally the platforms were approved and the nominees selected. The platforms included each party's position on all the critical issues. There was alignment, coherence, and focus in each platform, although they were driven by different visions, values, and priorities for action. The standard for picking the nominee in each party was that the candidate had to be able to sell the party platform to the American voters and implement it as president.

Over the years I have engaged in politics at the local, state, and national levels, and I have experienced dramatic changes in American politics that have had a significant impact on the way those running for public office must campaign and, once elected, govern. Now politics in America is driven by special interests and advocates who view a candidate's support on a single issue as the criterion that will determine whether the candidate receives both financial backing during the campaign and support from voters. The litmus test for candidates is their stance on each individual issue, not on a whole platform of key issues that government must address at the local, state, or national levels. At hundreds of school board and community meetings, in state legislative hearings, and in congressional hearings in Washington, I have experienced the enormous power of lobbying groups, the fundraising capacity of special interest advocates, the pressure of scorecards that are used to publicize the voting records of those elected, the public demonstrations at school board and other local community meetings, and the dissemination of interest group information using various communications media. The cumulative impact of the political process on the decision making of elected officials has become enormous. It is almost impossible for any elected official to ignore a special interest group.

District and school leaders and school board members must have the courage to make decisions that serve the best interests of children rather than attempt to accommodate advocacy groups who support the special interests of adults—which may conflict with what is right for children. These dramatic changes in politics require district and school leaders to have well-honed

> *District and school leaders and school board members must have the courage to make decisions that serve the best interests of children.*

skills in dealing with the realities of special interest politics, and the skill and courage to lead the charge in their districts, schools, and communities for recovering support for public education, because it is the essential ingredient for serving the common good and creating and sustaining a viable democracy.

How do district and school leaders do this? The first instinct is to resonate with the admonition that "all politics are local." Those who become leaders in communities where they have lived and worked do have an edge in understanding local politics in terms of who the opinion leaders are in the community and who the advocates and critics of the public schools are. They understand who runs for the local school board, city council, mayor, and other local offices. They also understand the importance of engaging families and the other adults who are important in the lives of students, the faith-based community, service clubs, business leaders, private and nonprofit community organizations, and others. And it is important to have a plan for how best to make these connections to inform these stakeholders of what the school's challenges and opportunities are and what it takes to address them, and to develop relationships with the leadership in these various sectors of the community. School board members often are affiliated with leaders in one or more of these sectors; they can be very helpful in keeping the superintendent informed about what they are seeing and hearing in the community—so long as their purpose is to think systemically about how the pieces of the puzzle come together and make the whole greater than the sum of its parts, rather than to leave to the superintendent the responsibility for doing so alone.

District and school leaders constantly face time management challenges. They will function well if they set priorities in terms of maximizing the value of how they spend their time in relation to meeting their responsibilities as leaders. Leaders coming from outside the district, region, or state will face the challenge of knowing how to set priorities during the first hundred days. The focus should be on listening and learning, spending as much time in schools as possible, and determining who the opinion leaders are in the community and scheduling meetings with them. For example, I would ask each board member to give me his or her individual list of who were the twenty most important people in the community, the twenty most important schools to visit, the twenty most important central office people to meet with, and the five most important issues he or she thought the school board should address during my first year. The number of people and schools it is possible to visit in those early weeks will vary depending on the size of the district and the number of schools. The point is to be intentional and to control the calendar and use of time in those early weeks in the new leadership position. And the patterns of overlap and connection from the individual lists will be very helpful in setting priorities.

From my Washington experience as assistant secretary for elementary and secondary education for two-and-a-half years of President Clinton's first term, I learned about transition teams and how to bridge the departure of a leader and the arrival of a new one. In the transition from my position in Washington to that of superintendent in Boston, I selected Bob Peterkin, a former superintendent in Cambridge and Milwaukee who was the director of the Urban Superintendents Program at the Harvard Graduate School of Education, to head the transition team. Early in his career, Bob served as a deputy superintendent in Boston and had deep knowledge of the school district. He convened a diverse group of about a dozen people from the district and community; they formulated a transition plan that represented their best thinking on what should be sustained and changed in BPS, the key issues I would face, suggestions for how to allocate my time during the first hundred days, the key people to be on my priority list for meetings, the political challenges and key players, and other bits of useful advice. This plan enabled me to begin on day one knowing how to plan my day and maintain control of a very transparent calendar, which resulted in the most successful entry I experienced as a superintendent.

Leaders in school districts and schools see themselves as educators. Most began their careers as classroom teachers, and many did so without aspirations for leadership roles beyond the classroom. However, they soon learned that the effective leadership of the principal was a critical factor in determining the quality of the school. Principals and central office staff have the same expectation for their superintendent. This chapter has addressed the skills school and district leaders must develop and use across the legal, political, and fiscal landscape to succeed in improving teaching and learning for all students in every school and classroom.

3

Serving Urban School Children

Janice E. Jackson

Knowing who is being served in urban schools is an essential first step in ensuring that the learning needs of all children will be met. A commitment to "leave no child behind" requires that we face the harsh realities of the contexts of the lives of many children in urban schools. There is significant research to suggest that too often in the United States, demography is seen as destiny (Orfield and Lee, 2007; Rothstein, 2008). This proposition need not be so. The public school can be a key institution in shifting what some assume to be inevitable.

The demographic landscape of urban schools has changed dramatically since 1983, when the clarion call to place our nation's struggling schools at the top of our political agenda was sounded. The National Commission on Excellence in Education expressed a concern for the long-term health of our economy if our public schools failed to raise the academic achievement of students. It has been interpreted by Orfield and Lee as a shift from a policy focus on equity to a focus on excellence, as though some leaders think the two could not coexist. This began a move away from the use of desegregation as a tool to improve access to a quality education for children of color. Schools across the country are experiencing a new wave of resegregation. The racial, ethnic, and class makeup of urban schools has changed in dramatic ways. There has been an increase in the number of black[1] and Latino children attending "segregated minority schools," defined as schools that are 90 to 100 percent nonwhite. Researchers have documented the social and economic costs of segregated schools post *Brown*. The shift in the racial and ethnic composition of schools is intertwined with the significant increase of children in poverty. Many of the social supports that existed in the pre–civil rights era have been eroded.

Racial and Ethnic Composition

According to Orfield and Lee (2007), in the late 1960s when many desegregation cases were crafted, white students made up 80 percent of the student population. By 2005 the shift was clear: white children were 57 percent of the student population, Latinos were 20 percent, blacks were 17 percent, Asians were 5 percent, and Native Americans were 1 percent. Demographers posit that the white student population will drop below 40 percent by the middle of this century. The composition in large urban environments was even more dramatic: Latino students, 38 percent; black students, 32 percent; white students, 22 percent; Asian students, 7 percent; and Native American students, 1 percent. In 2005, a closer look into schools in large urban areas provided a picture of 51 percent of students attending segregated minority schools, defined as having 90 to 100 percent students of color. In large urban districts, the percentage of white students in segregated white schools, defined as 90 to 100 percent white, is less than 1 percent. The numbers shift for midsize urban schools: 17 percent in segregated minority schools and 7 percent in segregated white schools. More than one-third of schools in large urban areas are "stably segregated minority schools," meaning that the schools

---

[1]The term *black* is used because many black Americans whose lineage was not from the early settlement of the country connect their identities to their families' countries of origin. Their families immigrated in a different era. They do not identify themselves as African American.

were 90 to 100 percent nonwhite in both 1995–96 and 2005–06. In midsize cities, only 9 percent were in this category. It is interesting to note that the number of "multiracial schools," defined as schools where students are from at least three racial and ethnic groups that each constitutes at least 10 percent of the total enrollment, make up 15 percent of schools nationally (Frankenberg, 2009). The racial and ethnic composition of schools varies by region of the country. The two regions experiencing the greatest growth between 1990 and 2005 are the West and the South. In the West, the share of white students dropped 14 percentage points; in the South, 9 percentage points (Orfield and Lee, 2007, p. 16).

Poverty

The increase of students of color in urban schools is coupled with a sharp increase in the number of students living in poverty. "Poverty has long been one of the central problems facing segregated schools. Segregation tends to be multidimensional. Few highly segregated minority schools have middle class student bodies. Typically students face double segregation by race/ethnicity and by poverty" (Orfield and Lee, 2007, p. 18). In January 2010, the National Center for Children in Poverty reported that 19 percent of children live in families that are considered poor based on the federal poverty level. Eight percent of children live in extremely poor families. Researchers have stated that the current poverty measure is too low. In fact, families need an income that is twice the federal poverty level to make ends meet. These families are referred to as "low-income." If that group were taken into account, 41 percent of the nation's children are living in families in poverty. The breakdown of poor children by race is as follows: 35 percent of black children, 31 percent of Latino and Native American children, 15 percent of Asian children, and 11 percent of white children. Low-income children are more likely to live in urban areas. Frankenberg (2009) found that nearly half of low-income students live in urban areas compared to 31 percent living in suburban areas. In urban areas, the poverty isolation is extreme. This is further complicated by the fact that in 2005, one out of fifteen children living in the United States was born outside the United States, and most were Latino. Unlike previous waves of immigration, in 2000 only 15 percent were from Europe, with over half coming from Latin America and a quarter from Asia (Nieto, 2005, p. 44). Frankenburg noted that though circumstances may vary, foreign-born students are more likely to live in poverty than native-born students. More than nine out of ten of both English language learners and second-generation immigrants attend urban schools (Fix and Capps, 2005, cited in Frankenberg, 2009, p. 261). Approximately 20 percent of all public school children speak a home language other than English. These children tend to be concentrated in schools with other English language learners. These schools are twice as likely to be in urban districts (Constentino de Cohen, Deterding, and Chu Clewell, 2005, cited in Frankenberg, 2009, p. 261).

Orfield and Lee (2007) found that in urban areas in 2006, two-thirds of black and Latino children attended schools where 75 percent of children lived in families that met the federal standards for free and reduced lunch (annual income of $21,580 for a family of three). Poor families face many hardships that have an indirect effect in schools. Many of these families face difficulties with obtaining enough food to eat, and even when there is enough, it is often not the healthiest of diets. Many low-income families spend more than 30 percent of their income on rent. Seventeen percent of poor children lack health insurance. Children living in poverty are often exposed to violence and crime, stress, and lack of employment and recreational opportunities. Contrary to popular belief, seven out of ten poor children are living in families where one person is working full- or part-time during some part of the year (Children's Defense Fund, 2008, p. 1).

Schools with large numbers of poor children tend to have less qualified and less experienced teachers, higher teacher turnover, and lower graduation rates. Researchers have found that students in urban classrooms are offered less challenging course work. Schools with larger numbers of children living in poverty experience high student mobility. Poor families find themselves changing residences for involuntary reasons, such as eviction, mortgage foreclosures, inability to pay the rent or utility bills, housing code enforcement, eminent domain actions, condominium conversions, upgrading rehabilitation, and other gentrification pressures (Hartman, n.d., p. 228). These disparities contribute to the achievement gaps that plague our nation's schools.

Low-Performing Schools: Effects of Poverty and Racism

"The extent to which a society utilizes its human potential is among the chief determinants of its prosperity" are the opening words of the McKinsey & Company report *The Economic Impact of the Achievement Gap in America's Schools* (2009, p. 5). This report documents four distinct achievement gaps that hold our children hostage: (1) between the United States and other nations, (2) between white students and black and Latino students, (3) between students of different income levels, and (4) between similar students schooled in different systems or regions. Children on the lower side of the gap are often *school-dependent children.* The Forum for Education and Democracy (2007) uses this phrase to refer to children who need school as a foundational place for their academic achievement and other basic needs. For these children, school must be a place where the adults take individual and collective responsibility for ensuring that they achieve to high levels. In many urban

> *Too often the life circumstances that surround these children are seen by school leadership and staff as insurmountable odds.*

schools, this is not the case. Too often the life circumstances that surround these children are seen by school leadership and staff as insurmountable odds against which they have little hope of moving all students forward. Too often the narrative in schools grows out of a deficit model. The beliefs that undergird the actions of the adults in the building are grounded in low expectations for the majority of children who sit before them. Teachers and principals do not come to these beliefs on their own. They are beliefs commonly held in our society about poor children, children of color, individuals whose first language is not English, and children who have special learning needs. The crisis arises when the very individuals charged with facilitating learning may not have the belief, knowledge, and skills needed to meet the responsibilities of their jobs. In a 2004–05 study by the Center for Strengthening the Teaching Profession, 92 percent of new teachers said they had received training in how to teach a diverse student population, but only 25 percent felt confident that they could actually do it. Over the last decade, the rhetoric in education has been to support the learning of all children who cross the schoolhouse door. In reality, not enough has been done to help teachers acquire the knowledge and skills needed to educate a population that has been traditionally underserved. Yet the mandate has been set into law.

Understanding the Inner Workings of Urban Schools

In 2006, the Education Trust posed the question, "How should schools respond to racism and poverty?" in its report *Yes We Can* (p. 3). Recognizing that there are many external influences on children's lives, the question called on educators to take an active role in continuing to make education a path to success and prosperity. Social research is rife with explanations for the gaps in achievement. The perception of many educators is that children of color who live in poverty do not have the same academic capacity as middle- and upper-class white students (Farkas, Grober, Sheehan, and Shaun, 1990, p. 128). For school-dependent children, teachers' expectations play a powerful role in their learning. Teachers' low expectations can reduce students' academic self-image, creating a self-fulfilling prophecy. Cooper posits that in the face of teachers' disbelief, school-dependent children can fall victim to attributional ambiguity (Crocker and Major, 1989, cited in Cooper, 2009) or stereotype threat (Steele and Aronson, 1995, cited in Cooper, 2009). Attributional ambiguity involves a dilemma that a student of a stigmatized group may face when receiving feedback about his or her performance. The student may wonder if the feedback is a result of his or her actual performance or if it is reflective of general racial bias on the part of the person giving feedback. Stereotype threat is the threat of being viewed through the lens of negative stereotypes, or the fear of doing something that might inadvertently confirm that stereotype.

Diamond, Randolph, and Spillane (2004) have demonstrated that the racial, ethnic, and socioeconomic composition of the student body is deeply coupled with the expectations teachers hold about children's capacity to achieve and the teachers' responsibility for supporting students' learning. They found that in predominantly low-income black schools, teachers emphasized students' deficits and had a reduced sense of responsibility for children's learning. They found in contrast that when a large proportion of the students were middle income, white, or Asian, students' intellectual assets were emphasized, and teachers felt more accountable for what students learned. The researchers suggest that teachers' sense of responsibility for learning outcomes for students is connected to their beliefs about students' academic abilities, beliefs grounded in a set of organizationally embedded expectations regarding what is possible for students from particular backgrounds. They use the term *organizational habitus* (Horvat and Antonio, 1999, cited in Diamond, Randolph, and Spillane, 2004, p. 76) to describe this phenomenon. Diamond and colleagues define organizational habitus as "class-based dispositions, perceptions, and appreciations transmitted to individuals in a common organizational culture." It is their contention that the micropolitical contexts of schools and classrooms should be a focus on actions taken to improve the achievement of students of color. Micropolitical context is the day-to-day interactions through which people value and make sense of difference. The micropolitical context is often influenced by the racial and social class composition of the student population. Diamond and colleagues see two features of micropolitical context in operation here—teachers' evaluation of students' ability and teachers' individual and collective sense of responsibility for students' learning.

Lee and Smith (2001, cited in Diamond, Randolph, and Spillane, 2004, p. 78) found that in schools with a high degree of collective responsibility for students' learning, achievement gains are greater. Collective responsibility has three components: (1) teachers' internalization of responsibility for students' learning, (2) their willingness to adapt teaching practices to students' needs, and (3) their sense of efficacy in their teaching practices. Diamond, Randolph, and Spillane (2004) studied schools with high collective responsibility. School leaders played a key role in shifting teachers from focusing on the challenges facing students to raising their expectations of themselves in helping children push past those obstacles. Perry (2003, p. 51) speaks of schools and communities providing a "counternarrative" to the pervasive story of students' lack of ability. The concept embraced by school leaders in places that are successful for disenfranchised children is that the individuals in the organization will work together to create an environment where the notion of success for all is the norm. The leadership intervenes in the regular conversations among teachers, shifting them away from a focus on the children's troubles and toward a conversation that is aware of the realities of children's lives but strives to build on students' social and cultural capital as well as their individual assets. These leaders make space for honest conversations and provide professional development to help teachers enhance their own practices to meet the needs of their students.

What's a School Community to Do?

Social science research is also filled with stories of school leaders and staff who had a strong conviction that it was their role to create a new course for children with challenging lives. These adults do not fall prey to low expectations for their students' performance. The Consortium on Chicago School Research partnered with Chicago Public Schools to study what went on in schools in response to the groundbreaking Chicago School Reform Act of 1988, which moved resources and authority away from the central office to the local school councils. The researchers and school personnel focused on the conditions that made success possible in many school communities. They were intrigued by the variation that occurred across elementary schools in Chicago. The work culminated in a focus on the schools as an organization and on the development of five essential categories of in-school supports that lead to improving student engagement and learning.

Leadership is the first support and is the foundation for the other four supports: parent-community ties, professional capacity of faculty and staff, a student-centered learning climate, and ambitious instruction (Sebring, Allensworth, Bryk, Easton, and Luppescu, 2006, p. 9). Leadership is distributed (Spillane, 2009, p. 70). Leadership is not seen as role based. It is relational and is supported by engaging all segments in the community in focusing on the needs of children. Although it may be easier in the short run to lead by fiat, it is better in the long run to engage the staff and community in key decisions about the school. The principal, the titular leader, is charged with keeping the school community's sights on instruction and student learning. His or her behavior and decisions must signal that the

Relation trust: an interrelated set of mutual dependencies that are embedded within the social exchanges in any school.

primary work of schools is to ensure that all students are engaged in rigorous learning. The principal must be unwavering in keeping instruction and student achievement at the core of all that happens in the school. The principal must have a deep understanding of how children and adults learn, and of curriculum, instruction, and assessment. He or she must have the knowledge and skill to facilitate teachers' continued learning and application of that learning to their own teaching practices. Finally, he or she must be able to provide teachers with the resources they need to carry out their responsibilities. The principal must be in classrooms regularly and have a deep understanding of how students are achieving across the school, for he or she sets the tone for the sense of collective responsibility for students' learning. The principal must believe in the staff's and the community's ability to address the challenges facing students.

The second support is the involvement of parents and others in the community. Too often the relationship between parents and schools is hampered by mistrust on both sides. Bryk and Schneider (2003) have done extensive research that demonstrates that schools with high relational trust show greater achievement gains for children. (The researchers describe relational trust as an interrelated set of mutual dependencies that are embedded within the social exchanges in any school. As individuals interact with one another, they are constantly discerning the intentions behind the actions of others. These discernments organize around four considerations: respect, personal regard, competence in core responsibilities, and personal integrity [pp. 41–42]).

The walls between families and schools must come down.

The walls between families and schools must come down. Bryk and Schneider (2003) saw that in successful schools, this pattern was broken.

Teachers were knowledgeable about student culture and the local community, and they drew on these lessons. They learned from parents about how they saw their own role in supporting their children's learning. Teachers were able to draw on children's knowledge to make connections to new content and concepts. School staff reached out to parents and community to engage them in strengthening their children's learning. They worked with parents and community members to show them specific things they could do with their children to support the academic content being taught in the classroom. Schools drew on a network of community organizations to improve services for children and families.

Professional capacity is the third essential support. In this work, professional capacity refers to the combination of human and social resources. It pertains to the quality of the staff, their beliefs about their role in bringing about and sustaining improvement, the quality of ongoing professional development, and the capacity of a staff to work collaboratively on improving teaching and learning. It is common knowledge that teachers need to be steeped in subject matter knowledge and equipped with a variety of strategies to meet students' learning needs as they engage them with depth of content and develop higher-order thinking skills. What is less often addressed is the importance of teachers' having a belief in their students' ability to master the material placed before them and a belief in their own knowledge and skill to be a catalyst to bring about success when the path is not obvious. Teachers' individual beliefs lay the groundwork for the shared beliefs that shape a sense of collective responsibility. Beliefs are often difficult to change. The focus should be on changes in behavior.

Quality professional development is one of the key conditions that support teachers in changing practice and pushing against the tide of beliefs that work against student learning. New knowledge, opportunities to practice the ideas that have been learned in professional development, feedback about implementation, exposure to stories of success that connect to their own experience, and reflection—alone and with others—are necessary for long-term changes in practice. The school, as an organization, should be in a problem-solving mode. This calls on teachers to open their practice to an audience beyond their students. Making their practice public is an emotionally difficult step for many teachers to take. Building a collaborative community in which the staff share ideas about teaching and learning, visit each other's classrooms, and raise questions and dilemmas about teaching requires purposeful facilitation over time.

The fourth essential support is a student-centered learning climate. Creating and maintaining a safe and orderly environment that is conducive to learning for students and staff is critical. Students need the adults in the building to make their expectations of them clear. Beyond order and safety is the need for *academic press*. There needs to be an atmosphere of high academic standards for all children coupled with the necessary instructional strategies and social supports.

The final support is ambitious instruction. All students should be engaged with a rigorous curriculum that challenges them to master basic knowledge and skills while pushing them to stretch their capacity to engage in complex and creative thinking. Faculty and leadership should recognize that the school is a complex organization that needs to ensure horizontal and vertical alignment for curriculum and instruction. Teachers of the same grade should be driving toward having students meet the same content and performance standards. Teachers across the school need a clear understanding about how the work in their classrooms is connected to the work in other grades. This requires ongoing schoolwide planning.

The work of the Consortium on Chicago School Research tracks nicely with the work by Diamond and colleagues (2004) that was mentioned earlier. The administration and faculty of a school need to see their work as collective and connected to the communities from which the children come. It is important that they continue to ask themselves, What do we need to know about the learning needs of our children? What do we need to know and do to meet those needs? When the needs are beyond our knowledge or skill level, who can assist us in responding appropriately? Schools do not exist in isolation; they are major institutions in a complex web of institutions.

A Story of Success

There are schools that serve as windows into what is possible. The Gardner Elementary School is one example. Faculty in the Lynch School of Education at Boston College initiated a partnership project with several schools in the Allston-Brighton area of Boston, which is contiguous to the university. The project began with a relationship between the principal of the Gardner Elementary School and a faculty member in the school of education. The partnership has mutual benefits for the university's faculty and students as well as for the Gardner Elementary School students, staff, and families. Over the years, this relationship blossomed into a much larger initiative involving the school, several faculty members and students from different parts of the university, and community agencies. It is now led by a steering committee comprising individuals representing the four prongs of the partnership—the school, the university, community agencies, and community coalitions. The initiative brings the partners together to address the academic and nonacademic needs of children. There are several projects going on in the partnership. The projects enable faculty and students to work alongside educators, families, and community agencies to address pressing needs within the community. One project that has shown great promise is the work at the Gardner Elementary School.[2]

---

[2]Information about this initiative was drawn from personal experience and Walsh et al., 2000.

In 2008–09, school enrollment at the Gardner Elementary School was roughly 350 students in grades K–5. It is located in a culturally and linguistically diverse section of Boston. At least thirty-six languages are spoken among the students and faculty. Eighty percent of the students participate in the free and reduced lunch program, and eighty percent of families have limited English proficiency.

The school is an Extended Services school that has an extended day for children while providing a range of services for children and their families. This model enables adults to attend to the wide variety of issues that impede students' learning. Teachers engage in professional development activities that are often co-led by university faculty and students as well as by staff from the school. There is a strong commitment to improve the capacity of the school staff to meet the needs of children over time. There is no sign of a quick fix. There is a commitment to dig in and grapple with the problems that present themselves so that meaningful and long-term solutions can be developed. The members of the initiative believe in their collective capacity to solve problems.

Meeting the academic needs of children is the primary work of schools. However, the members of this initiative recognize that learning does not occur when children and their families are struggling with physical health concerns, socioemotional issues, effects of poverty, and legal concerns. The partners did not come to this work easily. There was a need to get to know each other's strengths and challenges. The planning committee for this project consisted of members from the university, the school, the families, and the community agencies. By year two they had accomplished several things: (1) developed programs for children that took place before and after school as well as in the summer; (2) arranged for services beyond academics, such as dental and medical care, mental health care, and social services; (3) developed evening programs for parents and other adults, such as ESL, GED, immigration counseling, housing access, and health education; and (4) raised matching funds to support ongoing work.

The members of the partnership attribute their success to several factors: a shared theory of change, engagement in reflective practice, a long-term commitment on the part of partners, and a funding arrangement that balances the distribution of resources once acquired. Although there were issues to be worked out, such as governance and cultural differences of the various professionals, the group found a way to set egos aside and learn from and with each other.

> *Although there were issues to be worked out, . . . the group found a way to set egos aside and learn from and with each other.*

Conclusion

Much has changed in the student population. The need for a rigorous education for all students has not changed. In fact, it has become ever more important. The children of this nation are counting on us to place their best interest at the core of our work. We cannot turn a blind eye. Now is the time to step forward with courage and an unwavering commitment to ask and answer the tough questions that present themselves in public education.

References

Bryk, A., and Schneider, B. (2003). "Trust in Schools: A Core Resource for School Reform." *Educational Leadership, 60*(6), 40–44.

Children's Defense Fund. (August 26, 2008). *Child Poverty in America.* Washington, DC: Children's Defense Fund. http://www.childrensdefense .org/child-research-data-publications/data/child-poverty-in-america.pdf.

Cooper, E. (2009). "Realities and Responsibilities in the Education Village." In L. Tillman (ed.), *The SAGE Handbook of African American Education.* Thousand Oaks: Sage.

Diamond, J., Randolph, A., and Spillane, J. (2004). "Teachers' Expectations and Sense of Responsibility for Student Learning: The Importance of Race, Class, and Organizational Habitus." *Anthropology and Education Quarterly, 35*(1), 75–98.

Education Trust. (September 2006). *Yes We Can: Telling Truths and Dispelling Myths About Race and Education in America.* http://www.edtrust.org/dc/publication/yes-we-can-telling-truths-and-dispelling-myths-about-race-and-education-in-america.

Farkas, G., Grober, R., Sheehan, D., and Shaun, Y. (1990). "Cultural Resources and School Success: Gender, Ethnicity, and Poverty Groups Within an Urban District." *American Psychological Review, 55*(1), 127–142.

Forum for Education and Democracy. (March 15, 2007). *Guiding Principles for NCLB.* http://forumforeducation.org/node/100.

Frankenberg, E. (2009). "The Demographic Context of Urban Schools and Districts." *Equity and Excellence in Education, 42*(3), 255–271.

Hartman, C. (n.d.). *High Classroom Turnover: How Children Get Left Behind.* Washington, DC: Citizens' Commission on Civil Rights. http://www.cccr.org/Chapter16.pdf.

McKinsey & Company. (2009). *The Economic Impact of the Achievement Gap in America's Schools.* http://www.mckinsey.com/app_media/images/page_images/offices/socialsector/pdf/achievement_gap_report.pdf.

Nieto, S. (2005). "Public Education in the Twentieth Century and Beyond: High Hopes, Broken Promises, and an Uncertain Future." *Harvard Educational Review, 75*(1), 43–64.

Orfield, G., and Lee, C. (2005). *Why Segregation Matters: Poverty and Educational Inequality.* Cambridge, MA: Civil Rights Project, Harvard University.

Orfield, G., and Lee, C. (2007). *Historic Reversals, Accelerating Resegregation, and the Need for New Integration Strategies.* Los Angeles: Civil Rights Project, University of California. http://www.civilrightsproject.ucla.edu/research/deseg/reversals_reseg_need.pdf.

Perry, T. (2003). "Up from the Parched Earth: Toward a Theory of African-American Achievement." In T. Perry, C. Steele, and A. Hilliard (eds.), *Young, Gifted, and Black: Promoting High Achievement Among African-American Students* (pp. 1–108). Boston: Beacon Press.

Rothstein, R. (2008). "Whose Problem Is Poverty?" *Educational Leadership, 65*(7), 8–13.

Sebring, P., Allensworth, E., Bryk, A., Easton, J., and Luppescu, S. (2006). *Essential Supports for School Improvement.* Chicago: Consortium on Chicago School Research.

Spillane, J. (2009). "Managing to Lead: Reframing School Leadership and Management." *Phi Delta Kappan, 91*(3), 70–73.

Walsh, M., Brabeck, M., Howard, K., Sherman, F., Montes, C., and Garvin, T. (2000). "The Boston College-Allston/Brighton Partnership: Description and Challenges." *Peabody Journal of Education, 75*(3), 6–32.

4

Managing People

We all can remember outstanding teachers who were significant in shaping what we learned, understood, and were able to do as we developed through the stages of elementary, intermediate, high school, and postsecondary education. It is not unusual for us to reflect years later about the teachers who seemed to be tough, demanding, and even unfair. As adults we remember that in many different ways, our teachers made a significant and positive difference in our lives. For some of us, memories of the trips to the principal's office are not always pleasant, even though in hindsight we can understand the important role that principals have and how the most effective leaders set high expectations as they support the adults and students to shape and sustain high-performing schools. Research has confirmed our instincts about the importance of quality teaching in classrooms and leadership in schools. They are the two most important variables that the schools provide that make a difference in student achievement. And there are many other people in school districts and schools who provide essential support to enable teachers and principals to do their work. As noted earlier in the book, in most school districts 80 percent or more of the budget goes to salaries and benefits, and in schools the percentage typically is over 90 percent. This chapter focuses on leading and managing people (human capital), and how school district and school leaders can seize the opportunities and address the challenges discussed. It addresses preparation and certification, recruitment, sourcing (hiring and placement), induction, retention and tenure.

Preparation Programs

Traditionally, most teachers, principals, and school district leaders in America are trained in programs offered in undergraduate colleges and universities, university graduate schools of education, or alternative programs offered by various providers, which include private nonprofit organizations and, more recently, a few urban school districts. The goals of these programs are to prepare students to meet the state requirements for certification, acquire content knowledge for the relevant grade levels, and develop the skills required to become effective teachers with the support of knowledgeable and capable school leaders. There is widespread variation in the time allocated for course work, which focuses on acquisition of content knowledge (what teachers and leaders need to know and be able to do), and clinical practice in classrooms and schools, which enables aspiring teachers and leaders to learn how to be effective in their respective roles. Elementary school teachers must master content in a variety of subjects and gain a solid understanding of how to teach reading and mathematics so as to build a strong foundation for students in the primary grades, before they move into the upper elementary grades, where the focus shifts from learning to read to reading to learn. Teachers in middle and high schools typically are trained to focus on one major content area; they may also go into a second area with the goal of meeting certification requirements in more than one area, which will enable them to be more competitive in seeking teaching positions.

Traditionally principals were expected to be good managers. Their work focused on operations—establishing schedules, ordering materials, attending to school climate and discipline, accepting teachers assigned by the central office, conducting teacher evaluations once or twice a year for new teachers and once every two or three years for tenured teachers, completing reports on faculty and student attendance, filing updates on budget expenditures and participation rates in school breakfast and lunch programs, requesting adjustments in bus schedules, and pleading for the maintenance department to respond to work orders that require immediate attention. The role of principals began to change significantly in the early 1990s as standards-based reform gained traction and shifted expectations toward having all students, not just some, meet high standards of achievement and graduate from high school ready for postsecondary education or careers. District and school leaders were tasked with increasing responsibility to improve learning outcomes, which requires central office staff to align the curriculum and standards and work with principals to help teachers adjust and improve their teaching. They had to become instructional leaders and know how to support the improvement of teaching that would lead to successful learning for all students. The ripple effect has resulted in new ways of thinking about the focus of programs that train school leaders, and the professional development that school district leaders provide for principals.

Pre-Service Training

Preparation programs for teachers and school leaders too often focus more on curriculum and the content of teaching and leadership rather than on the dimensions of effective teaching and why both teachers and leaders must have a shared understanding of what good instruction looks like. This does not mean that there is a single definition of good instruction. However, school districts and schools should engage educators in conversations about what effective teaching is and how to observe and recognize it in schools and classrooms. The Boston Public Schools (BPS) spent more than a year engaging teachers, principals, central office staff, and others in a discussion to determine the "dimensions of effective teaching," which were adopted by the Boston School Committee. It is essential for preparation programs to understand how standards-based reform has raised expectations for student learners and the quality of instruction in every classroom and school where teachers will teach and principals will lead.

As the demographics continue to change in America's districts and schools, it is necessary to ensure that preparation programs for teachers and school and district leaders address the issues of diversity, race, and class. Not only are America's cities becoming more diverse, with families and students who have come to the United States from countries around the world, but the suburban rings surrounding cities are experiencing demographic shifts. And the percentages of low-income families living in these areas, as well as in rural areas, continue to change. The preparation programs for teachers and leaders offered by colleges and universities have not been known for their attention to the issues of race and class as a necessary and important part of their curriculum that should be aligned with the type of learning required during the clinical experience in schools and school districts. Most medical schools understand that the training of doctors would not be comprehensive without time spent in a city hospital with experiential learning in settings with diversity of race and class. The required course work for aspiring teachers, regardless of where they may teach, should include learning about race and class, how they see these issues through the lens of their own races and classes, and how they can better understand how others who are different from them may see them. Addressing this subject requires difficult conversations and often makes people uncomfortable. However, if they are going to realize the important goals of having all students reach high standards and of closing achievement gaps that exist among groups where race and class are significant and important variables, leaders in school districts and schools must be able to model behavior and lead the tough conversations about how to serve all children well.

What are some promising strategies for school district and school leaders to use to improve pre-service teacher training? Partnerships with higher education institutions; entrepreneurial organizations, such as Teach for America and New Leaders for New Schools; charter management organizations; teacher and leader residency programs created by urban school districts; and other alternative certification programs are important. They supply most of the training that aspiring teachers and leaders must complete to qualify for state certification, and some have effectively embraced the opportunity to create a market dynamic of competition and choice, which provides opportunities for innovation and change.

Location of preparation programs has been a challenge. One issue is that for years, student teachers were placed in classrooms with teachers who graduated from the same programs. In large districts, often there was little knowledge of how many student teachers were in the district and where they were assigned. Teachers in schools often maintained contact with their teacher training programs, and principals had to agree to accept the student teacher but often did not have the flexibility to determine the placement because the programs insisted on placing the student teacher with one of their graduates. A second issue is that given the culture of isolation in most schools, where teachers are expected to be in their classrooms with their own students for most of the day, there are limited opportunities for collaboration and shared learning among classrooms with teachers and their student teachers. Third, rural school districts located great distances from the preparation programs find it more difficult to attract student teachers without housing. The good news is that advances in technology are helping create effective ways to provide distance learning.

What are some new ways of thinking about pre-service training? District leaders can set some ground rules for the clinical experience. For example, they can cluster student teachers in schools where there is strong interest and capacity evident

in the school leaders and staff to provide a robust clinical experience for the student teachers; this approach is similar to that used
in a teaching hospital. The teacher training program would be
expected to assign a staff member to the school site, spending a significant amount of time based on the number of student teachers
assigned to the school. The principal would seize the opportunity
to find ways to get the supervising and student teachers to work
together and to engage with the rest of the staff. The incentive
for both experienced and novice teachers who best demonstrate
their commitment to collaboration and succeed in working
together to improve the learning experience for all students would
be a continuing teacher-leader role for the experienced teacher and
a teaching position the following year for the novice. The novice
as a first-year employee and the teacher-leader who was his or
her mentor would continue their collaboration. In schools where
there are several student teachers, there is the opportunity to
continue this model of collaboration with teams. The principal's
commitment to both collaboration and support for teams to
convene and work together is essential. Moreover, the preparation programs must understand how important it is to encourage
and support change in school culture and how to prepare teachers
and principals to work in teams and embrace collaboration and
shared learning. To succeed, this model requires ongoing commitment to change and improvement from teacher preparation programs, school districts, and schools.

With the advancements of technology, particularly in districts
and schools where there is not close access to college and university teacher training programs, it is possible to create an online
option for the student to continue some course work and to spend
a full quarter or semester on-site at a school that is not within
easy travel time of the teacher training program. We can expect
increasing numbers of students who will be learning part-time or
full-time through virtual schools. This will not eliminate the need
for excellent teachers who will in turn teach aspiring teachers,

but it will require changes in the ways we think about teaching and learning for adults as well as students. Using technology to record and observe accomplished school leaders and classroom teachers in real time, as well as novices engaged in their clinical experiences in schools, will help address the challenges of access as well as reinforce the necessity of focusing on what the qualities of effective teaching and differentiated instruction look like. Reading about the dimensions of effective teaching and leadership is important but not sufficient. Observation of effective practice is an essential component in preparing teachers and leaders.

Certification for Teachers and Leaders

Certification requirements are established by the states and play a major role in shaping the courses and content of teacher and leader preparation programs. Most states require teachers, principals, superintendents, and other central office staff to obtain certification, which presumably is tailored to reflect the skills required for the positions. Traditionally the required trajectory of experience begins in the classroom, which becomes a prerequisite for leaders qualifying to become administrators in schools and is a requirement to serve in central office administrative positions or become a superintendent. This trajectory has shaped certification requirements that primarily are course focused. Although there is reciprocity and acceptance of certificates among some states, educators who want the opportunity to work in several different states during their careers are confronted with additional course-based certification requirements in states where reciprocity does not exist.

My experience serving as a superintendent in five states in different regions of the country required me to complete at least one additional course to meet superintendent certification requirements each time. I was surprised by the variety in courses required, unclear about how they related to the role of the superintendent of schools, and bemused by the reluctance to accept evidence of experience doing the things the courses presumably taught to grant a waiver for the courses. For example, in one state, a course for teaching elementary school reading was required. I had never taken a course in teaching elementary reading. My teaching experience was in junior and senior high school. I had served as a superintendent in several other states and been responsible for leading staff in the decision-making process to adopt reading programs for schools, but that experience did not count. In another state, I was required to take a course in special education policy. I had previously served as superintendent in two other states, worked extensively with special education programs in those districts, and was quite familiar with federal and state policy for students with disabilities. The irony was that I knew more about special education policy than the teacher who taught the course I was required to take at a local university; further, the course used a single dated textbook and true-false or multiple-choice tests to determine what we were learning. Only a year earlier, the first significant federal legislation had been passed setting policy for what states and school districts were required to do to meet the needs of students with disabilities. I was leading an urban district with forty-five thousand students and a substantial special education population. We were already implementing the new federal requirements.

In some states, the quality of the certification requirements has improved. For example, there is recognition of the importance of having those who seek certification demonstrate their knowledge and application of it on required state exams, generally in English language arts and mathematics and, in some states, on tests in the subjects teachers will teach. However, certification tests do not generate data that provide qualitative evidence about the candidates' teaching or leadership skills; this is a shortcoming that must be addressed as school and district leaders approach the challenges of recruitment.

Alternative routes to certification have gained traction in recent years and have become an important element as district and school leaders think about the recruitment and hiring of teachers, principals, central office leaders, and superintendents. Without the innovative approaches

> *Without the innovative approaches provided by high-quality alternative routes to certification, there would be fewer aspiring teachers and school leaders.*

provided by high-quality alternative routes to certification, there would be fewer aspiring teachers and school leaders willing to enter the profession. My own experience has been shaped by pathways to teaching and leadership that resulted not just from alternative approaches to certification but from the ways in which those who trained teachers and leaders thought about nontraditional approaches in the design of courses and about the ways in which adults learn; they created different venues for learning to take place, thus providing more opportunities for clinical experience. They were not bound by school settings that accepted the default culture of isolation and atomization, where structures like egg crates separate teachers, who expect to spend a full day in their classrooms doing the best they can with the students assigned, and where collaboration and shared learning are feared. Even the schools with redesigned groupings of open classrooms with few walls were short-lived because they did not convince many teachers, school leaders, or parents that schools without individual classrooms in the egg-crate structure were conducive to focused and successful instruction and student learning without distractions.

Hiring Strategies for Urban School Districts and Schools

There is not a simple one-size-fits-all strategy for successful recruitment of teachers or of school district and school leaders. There are many questions that recruiters and applicants will want answered. Here are a few examples of what applicants will be thinking about:

- Location is a high priority for me. Am I place bound, or am I willing to move? If I don't want to move, how far from where I live am I willing to travel to the school or school district where I will be working?

- Is the size of the community, school district, and school important?

- What are the demographics in the school district and schools where I want to work?

- Do I want to work in an urban, suburban, or rural area?

- Will I be more comfortable in a district and school serving middle-class students and families or where there is diversity of race and class?

- Is it possible that one or two friends and I could apply as a team to work in the same district or school?

- Do I have to live in the school district where I am a teacher or leader?

- What is a typical schedule for a teacher or school leader, and will I have scheduled planning time during the day?

Working conditions are important variables too, and recruiters should be ready to address them. Most of the examples focus on teachers, but many are also applicable to recruitment of school leaders or central office employees:

- Class size and the total number of students one is required to teach each day

- Official length of the school year and work day

- Professional development and opportunities for advancement

- Availability of necessary supplies and materials

- Types of supervision, support, and evaluation

- Characteristics of the district and school culture

- Reputation of the principal, school board, and superintendent

- Information on what happened to the previous principal and department head

- Compensation, benefits, and opportunities for additional work and compensation

- Policies for evaluation, accountability, and performance management

- Availability and use of technology

- The most challenging issues the school district and schools faced last year

- Rules governing tenure

- Type and duration of the employment contract

- Mentors assigned to new employees

- Union membership requirements

- Timelines and decision-making processes for hiring

Recruiters who are successful in finding and hiring the best applicants are well informed and ready to address the questions and areas of interest applicants will have, and are prepared to follow up with applicants when responses require additional information that the recruiter does not have at the time. Effective recruiters convey clear expectations, are transparent in providing information, and show respect for the applicant's concerns and need to know. Paying attention to these characteristics can make an important difference in getting the best applicants to accept offers of employment.

There are other variables that may be position specific. A candidate for superintendent will expect to have

- Access to school district data and a strategic plan if one exists
- Detailed information about the school board, such as the length of members' terms and years of service as board members
- Board-adopted policy documents
- Information about the board and superintendent relationships during the previous administration
- Data on the financial condition of the district, with the focus on existing and anticipated budget challenges
- Relationships with the press and other elected local, state, or national officials in the school district

A similar list would reflect what principal candidates need to know. The focus would be both on expectations for the role of principal that apply across the district in all schools and on expectations that are particular to the school where the opening exists. Certainly compensation plans that address salaries and benefits and other perks are important variables in attracting, hiring, and retaining the most effective people to school districts, schools, and classrooms, but these other variables should not be underestimated. They are essential in cultivating interest among the best candidates and convincing them to apply, pass paper screening, and become strong prospects for the applicant pool to be interviewed. These are not intended to be all-inclusive lists, but they should be considered as school districts and schools develop their recruitment strategies and specific plans for targeting recruits for specific positions. And there may be some elements that are viewed by some applicants as value added and by others as a reason to withdraw, such as pay for performance. Perhaps the most important issue for principals and superintendents is the confiden-tiality of the process and that there be no release to the public of the applicant pool, at least until the two or three finalists for the position are identified.

How will the people whom the district is trying to recruit get information and answers to their questions? There must be a good marketing plan. School boards have the responsibility for recruiting and hiring superintendents. Most conduct searches that will attract multiple applicants from inside and outside the school district. Some districts where there are one or several qualified internal candidates for the position may conduct their own selection pro-cess, identify candidates, conduct interviews, check references, and make a decision. The standard approach is to hire a search firm to conduct regional and national searches for candidates; develop a marketing strategy, and plan for outreach to recruit, screen, and form an applicant pool; develop an interview list for the board; and manage the process for the board—conducting reference checks and preliminary interviews, facilitating the board's process for determining finalists and reaching a decision, and creating a plan for announcement of the board's selection.

Human resource (HR) departments in most school districts are responsible for recruiting other school district employees, including central office staff, school leaders, teachers, and other employees assigned to schools. The HR lead position is now one of the most important senior leadership positions in school districts. The competition to find and hire skilled candidates is challenging. In some districts, internal candidates who have been successful teachers and principals move into the lead role in HR. Large dis-tricts now look to the private, nonprofit, and military sectors for leaders with impressive HR leadership experience and results.

It was in BPS, my fifth district as a superintendent, that I encountered my most challenging HR issues and made the most significant changes and improvements to address them. Through most of my career, HR departments were back-office operations.

The strategies for recruiting applicants were basic. Advertising in newspapers or journals was expensive. Sending notices of open positions to schools of education for posting on bulletin boards was cost-effective. Student teachers were easy to reach and interview, with numerous teacher training programs offered by many colleges and universities in Boston and its metropolitan area. The exception was the hard-to-fill fields—mathematics, science, special education, and English as a second language.

The queue provided applicants for most other school-level positions, such as department heads, counselors, assistant principals, principals, and central office positions. The queue was part of the culture in many school districts and schools where advancement was determined by longevity in the system rather than by evidence that a candidate had the qualities necessary to perform and succeed in the new position. Outsiders were hard to recruit. It was expensive, and as long as there were sufficient applicants from inside the school or school district, there was little incentive to search elsewhere, particularly if applicants would have to move to Boston, were vested in another state's retirement system, and were apprehensive about the cost of living in Boston and its metropolitan area. For those who were serving as leaders in suburban districts, the salaries were generally equal to or higher than those in BPS, where the leadership challenges are generally more complex than in suburban districts.

What had resulted in significant change, particularly in urban and suburban school districts in metropolitan areas, was the competition for candidates to serve in positions where supply did not meet demand. And even more important was the availability of the Internet and increasingly sophisticated technology that has enabled school districts and schools to use Web sites, streamed video, webinars, and other approaches to marketing, as well as videoconferencing and Skype for interviews.

Several strategies that helped improve our marketing for BPS was the regular updating of our Web site to improve its quality and ease of access. We also located a small street-level office immediately inside the entrance to the school district building; it had several computers, video messages, brochures, instructions for applying online, and Web site information, and was staffed by Human Resources Department employees who rotated shifts during regular working hours to assist walk-in candidates in learning about BPS. Interested candidates could also schedule interviews. A second strategy was to seek pro bono support from a communications and public relations agency, which helped us develop a branding and marketing program that improved our recruitment and hiring.

Other HR Challenges

Leaders in school districts and schools must never forget that it is the people in them who are the organizations' most valuable assets. There must be an organizational commitment to address the challenges that confront the HR departments in school districts. Although there may be year-to-year fluctuations in the number of applicants for specific positions, a review of previous years is likely to reveal patterns that can help project the challenges and opportunities for recruiting the best applicants in the current year. The hard-to-fill positions must be identified early in the hiring cycle, soon after the current school year begins. The data from past recruiting seasons should be scrubbed to determine where to focus early recruiting, when to hold district on- and off-site recruiting fairs, what changes to expect in enrollments and retirements for the next year, what is known about the budget and finance projections for the next year, and what the pool of potential applicants is for positions where internal candidates are ready for moves— for example, assistant principals and principals within the school district who might request a lateral move or be assigned to lead low-performing turnaround schools or a new schools. Other positions will be posted and advertised to recruit outside candidates.

There may be in-district training programs that have graduates who are ready for placement. Principals leading schools with teachers in the residency program tend to keep them after their residency ends if a position is open because they know from seeing a resident's work that they are getting a first-year teacher who has a year of experience; knows the school, faculty, and students; and is more experienced than many second-year teachers.

One of the biggest challenges for school HR office recruiters is timelines established by school board policy or union contracts, which set specific dates on the calendar for teachers to request and be considered for transfers to other schools, and for when teachers who are returning from leaves of absence are moved to an excess status because enrollment has dropped at a school, curriculum has been changed, or electives or other programs have been dropped. The timing of the transfer cycle is such that in some districts, the assigning of teachers who are in the excess pools may not be completed until late spring. This practice is more typical in urban than suburban school districts, which means that suburban districts are able to offer contracts to teachers several months before the urban districts are able to do so.

Teacher and Principal Residency Programs

The standard process for identifying potential school leaders, particularly in large urban school districts, has been for aspiring leaders to complete the required state certification, which in turn qualifies them for a spot in their school district's leadership queue, a place where they expect to wait for their time to come to step into leadership roles. Priority for selection is defined by seniority and time spent in line rather than capacity to do the work. Vestiges of this approach still exist in some school districts. However, the evidence from research and practice makes the compelling case for selecting capable leaders who know how to hire and support effective teachers who will make a positive difference in the learning of all students they teach. Successful principals must be effective instructional leaders as well as good managers.

In many ways, the trajectory of my career as a leader followed a nontraditional pathway. It would not have happened without the support of others who did not believe that time in position was the essential variable for determining leadership potential. In short, I taught for two years in an inner-city junior high school, returned to the Harvard Graduate School of Education for two years, and was introduced to the superintendent of the New Orleans Public Schools, who hired me as his administrative assistant, which was my first major leadership role. It lasted for two years, which was time enough to convince me that my long-term goal was to be a superintendent in a major urban school district. The improbable next step was the opportunity to apply for the position of superintendent in a small suburban Philadelphia school district, with forty-five hundred students, eight schools, and a nine-member elected school board. One of my graduate school professors, a former big-city superintendent, encouraged the board to interview me, and much to my surprise, several months before my twenty-ninth birthday I began my career as a superintendent, which ended thirty-seven years later after serving as superintendent in Eugene, Oklahoma City, San Diego, and Boston.

We now face a period where we should be thinking in new ways about career pathways to leadership positions in schools and school districts. Schools and school districts can no longer expect that they can staff their schools with teachers and leaders who will commit on the first day of their entry to a thirty-plus-year career in the same school or school district with the same guarantees for a 180-day school year, options to teach for a few weeks of summer school, a defined-benefit pension plan, and other benefits. This does not mean that there are not options to attract others to

> *We now face a period where we should be thinking in new ways about career pathways to leadership positions in schools and school districts.*

the profession if we are willing to think differently about changing and improving the structures, systems, and culture in our
schools and school districts. Currently there are nontraditional
pathways to teaching and leadership roles in school districts and
schools. Most have been created by those who believe in choice
and competition and are energized by the opportunity to innovate
and challenge the status quo.

Teacher residency programs are getting traction and provide one
compelling example of a new way of thinking about how to combine
the most effective methods for recruiting and preparing teachers and
principals for challenging roles in school districts and schools. At
the outset there can be controversy when a school district decides
to offer its own preparation programs for teachers and principals—
programs with alternative routes to certification and incentives that
attract teacher candidates who have backgrounds in the hard-to-fill
fields, and aspiring principals who are willing to lead in challenging schools. This controversy was present when the Boston Teacher
Residency (BTR) program began. Other preparation programs
offered by colleges and universities that control the market often do
not appreciate having to compete with a local school district.

BTR designs its own program consistent with state alternative
certification options; determines the curriculum for the program;
recruits nationally; encourages people of color to apply; offers
incentives that are attractive and cost-effective (for example, BTR
provides an $11,000 stipend for the yearlong teacher residency
program and a $10,000 forgivable loan for residents who success-
fully complete the program and teach a minimum of three years
in the school district); and partners with a local university that
agrees to offer credit toward a master's degree for courses taught
in the teacher residency program. BTR begins with a rigorous six-
week, course-based summer program, followed by a residency with
an accomplished teacher in a school four days a week for a full
school year, with Fridays for the continuation of course work. The
program started with 15 residents and expanded each year with

the goal of capping the program at 125 residents per year when it was taken to scale. By the 2009–10 school year, the program had grown to 80 residents per year and was held at that number because of the recession and budget cuts.

The Principals Fellows Program (PFP) created in the Boston Public Schools follows a pattern similar to the BTR. The major difference is the amount of the stipend, which approximates the Fellows' then-current salaries when they enter the yearlong program; the program enrolls ten to twelve Fellows each year.

With six years of data now available, the BTR and PFP results are very encouraging. Many large urban school districts lose high percentages of teachers in the first three to five years of their employment. The average loss is 50 percent by the end of year five. BTR program graduates have a retention rate close to 90 percent during their first three years, which is what is required to have their $10,000 loan forgiven. The retention rates for the fourth and fifth years are very encouraging as well: 80 to 85 percent. Other favorable indicators include dual certification, with many residents adding special education certification to their math, science, or English language learner certification. Each class of BTR residents has included at least 50 percent people of color, which reinforces the school district's commitment to having a diverse workforce.

The traditional teacher education programs in the Boston area are learning that BTR is not adversely affecting their enrollments, because it is focusing on the hard-to-fill fields and diversity, with which the major higher education institutions have struggled. It has also caused other programs to review their curricula and learn what is necessary to better prepare their students to work in urban school districts with high concentrations of low-income students and students of color. They are also looking at how to better balance the time spent in college and university course learning in relation to clinical training in school districts and schools where they hope to teach.

The BTR one-year program—which, as noted earlier, includes four full-time days per week in a school for the whole school year—provides the opportunity to learn, teach, and join a community of residents and their teachers in the schools. In addition, these groups of experienced teachers and residents are gaining the value added of learning from each other and changing the default culture of isolation, which is present in most schools, to a professional culture of collaboration and shared learning.

Assignment

I learned about assignments (the grade levels, courses, students, and other duties teachers are given) the hard way when I was looking for my first teaching position. In 1963, there were a few school districts on the West Coast recruiting teachers on the East Coast. I had three offers from city school districts in San Diego; Portland, Oregon; and Tacoma, Washington. My wife was offered an elementary teaching position at an independent school for girls that did not require teacher certification, so we moved to Tacoma. I had been promised a position teaching history at one of the high schools, but I was dismayed to learn on the opening day for new teachers that there were no high school history positions available, and I had been assigned to an inner-city junior high school to teach social studies.

When I reported for my first day, the principal greeted me and said I had been assigned from the central office and that he had never had anyone from the East Coast in his school. However, he said he would give me a good deal and assign me to teach only four classes rather than five and to spend an hour every day supervising students in the lunch room. The next surprise occurred on the first day of classes, when I learned that I would be teaching twenty-five students with disabilities the last period of the day. In 1963, students with moderate disabilities were grouped together and assigned to regular classes. I had no training that prepared me for meeting their needs and no assistance other than what I gleaned from colleagues who had the same group of students earlier in the day.

My first weeks were very challenging. There was no induction program. My colleague in the lunch room was very helpful in getting me started without too many missteps, and a science teacher on my floor became my unofficial mentor and friend. At the end of the year, I met with the principal to review my evaluation. He told me that I had done a good job. I respectfully reminded him that he had only opened my classroom door and peeked in a few times but had never observed my teaching. His response was that he knew what was going on in his school and that because I was effective in the lunch room where he had observed my work, I would have the same assignment in year two.

This story did have a happy ending because I learned how to work with diverse racial groups, most of whom were from low-income or working-class families. As I mentioned earlier in this book, I learned a great deal from my students with special needs—much more than they probably learned from me during my two years at the school. I owe them a debt of gratitude because they helped me become a better teacher as I began to understand that although many were capable of doing challenging work, others needed more support, which would later be called differentiated instruction. I also was able to develop relationships with students in the lunch room and as an assistant baseball coach after school, which made it much easier to deal with management challenges in the classroom, particularly with my special needs students.

Assignment still creates many challenges in school districts and schools. Most principals want to participate in hiring their teachers and expect to be held accountable for their decisions. They do want help with recruitment. With online applications becoming the norm, providing principals with direct access to hundreds of resumes, it is possible for them to identify promising prospects and reach out to them directly. This system can also be overwhelming and time-consuming. When HR departments are staffed to review applications, conduct screening interviews, and create lists of candidates worth pursuing, principals will still be able to decide which prescreened candidates to pursue as they compete with their colleagues to hire the best, particularly when there is a small applicant pool for the hardest-to-fill positions.

There is a connection between recruitment and assignment. Vacancies in existing schools have to be identified before positions can be posted; there are also new positions that result from opening new schools or starting new programs in existing schools. Class size policies approved by school boards or required by collective bargaining agreements will affect assignments. Enrollment projections are a critical factor. Schools with larger enrollments than projected will require additional staff that may have to be reassigned from underenrolled schools soon after the start of the school year. The principal's opportunity to select and assign is usually limited in this situation because a teacher is entitled to a position and must be placed in a school where vacancies exist and there is a match with the certification he or she holds. The same restrictions apply when teachers have been bumped from a school because of shifts in enrollment or elimination of programs, or where collective bargaining contracts provide them the option of moving without using the normal transfer process. The central office has the final responsibility for assigning those who are in the unassigned pool of employees who are tenured or have rights defined by collective bargaining contracts, state laws, or local school board policies, whether they are teachers or in other positions in the school district. If the district has employees who serve at will and are not covered in other ways, their positions will not be guaranteed. The superintendent, the HR leader, and those central office leaders who supervise principals must work together to resolve the assignment challenges when there are unfilled positions or displaced teachers who must be reassigned after the school year begins.

There are a variety of ways to develop partnerships between central office HR departments and the schools. The major tasks of the central office are to focus on recruitment and establish a high-quality applicant pool, work with other departments on induction programs, engage principals in hiring and assignment decisions, and coordinate the system of evaluation of all employees in the school district and schools. One effective model for site-based involvement in hiring in BPS is a three-person committee that includes a parent selected by the school site council, a teacher selected by the teachers in the school, and the principal. They interview candidates for teacher and other positions in the school and strive for consensus on whom to hire. Consensus is the norm. If it is not reached, the principal does have veto power, but it is rarely used.

The selection and assignment of principals are the most important personnel decisions superintendents make. The principal selection process in BPS has several steps. The first is to develop a qualified pool of candidates. The Principal Residency Program is the major strategy for developing qualified applicants. A second strategy is to expand the role of assistant principals beyond the narrowly defined set of typical tasks, such as discipline and operations, to include engagement in the selection of teachers and in their professional development and evaluation, which prepares them to become qualified and certified candidates for the role of principal. The second step is to create a process that engages staff and parents at the school in selecting candidates from the applicant pool to interview. The deputy superintendent who supervises the school convenes the site selection committee, which includes parents, teachers, and community members. The committee reviews resumes, decides whom to interview, and selects three unranked finalists for the superintendent to interview. Together the superintendent and deputy interview the finalists and decide to appoint one of the finalists to the position. If they are dissatisfied with the quality of the finalists, the superintendent will make the decision to appoint someone else. With few exceptions, this process determines the selection and assignments of principals. The engagement of parent, teacher, and administrator representatives in the selection process leads to a more seamless transition for the chosen principal.

Induction and Staff Support

Induction for new employees in school districts and schools should focus on helping teachers and leaders make a smooth transition to their new positions. In my experience, most school districts at best provide one or two days of orientation for teachers and principals, with a focus on important logistical issues related to salary, benefits, certification, personnel policies, position requirements, and responses to questions from the gathered group of new employees. Some school districts require new employees to attend orientation sessions without pay. Others provide a stipend to acknowledge the time commitment of the new employees and to convey the message of appreciation for the employees joining the school district and the importance of the work they will be doing in their respective roles. Many school districts understand the value added in providing more extensive and substantive programs for new teachers and principals during the first year of employment.

Rarely do superintendents and other district leaders have access to a formal induction program. One new program is the Superintendents Academy, funded by the Broad Foundation, which has a first-year support program for academy graduates when they are selected as superintendents in urban school districts. The superintendent has an executive coach who spends fifteen days in the district with the superintendent during year one. A strategic support team convened by the executive coach with two other experienced urban superintendents spends a weekend with the new superintendent after the first three months on the job, to assess the effectiveness of the entry plan and to discuss strategic planning and execution for the months ahead. Funding for audits to determine the strengths and weaknesses in such areas as budget and finance, curriculum, HR, and communications are available during the first few months of the superintendent's first year.

Induction programs may have both district- and site-based components. Principals and teachers in districts with common curriculum are able during a three- to five-day program to engage with district staff who support curriculum, instruction, and professional development in the schools. In districts with racial and class diversity, the district may provide diversity training, which is essential for employees who have not had experience with diversity. Time can be allotted for new teachers and their principals to interact during planned breakout sessions. This provides continuing and new principals with the time to work together before the official school year starts at the school sites.

Other approaches to induction include online access for new employees to review information that will be important for them to have before beginning their work. Access to the school Web site will be useful for those new employees who will be in schools; central office Web sites will be helpful to the new employees working there. New employees can e-mail questions to a designated site; the district assigns responsibility to a knowledgeable employee to acquire the necessary information to respond.

Once the new employee begins work, it is important to assign as a mentor an experienced employee in the central office who has good interpersonal skills, expertise in the work of the department, and interest in helping new employees make the transition to a new workplace. Schools use a variety of approaches to mentor new teachers and other school employees. The most common approach with teachers is to assign as a mentor an experienced colleague who teaches the same subject as the new secondary school teacher or grade level as an elementary teacher. The challenge for the principal is to schedule time for the mentor to be in the new teacher's classroom and for the new teacher to have time to observe the mentor's teaching. All too often, scheduling barriers prevent this kind of contact, which diminishes the effectiveness of the mentoring program.

Common planning time for the new teacher and mentor can be helpful, particularly if other teachers are willing to have the new teacher and mentor observe their teaching. The principal should be engaged in the process and make every effort to help find solutions to the barriers that make collaboration difficult. Videotapes of classroom instruction may be used to inform the learning of the new teacher and mentor. From personal observations and video coverage of classes, the principal can gain insight into the common challenges teachers are facing and those that are unique to an individual teacher. The data can help determine the focus for school-based professional development.

An effective use of resources is to identify a cadre of classroom teachers who have demonstrated success in teaching diverse populations of students to achieve at high levels, and to assign them for several years to full-time staff developer positions, with each supporting twelve to fifteen first-year teachers. This approach provides significant time for observation, demonstration lessons, consultations, support for lesson planning, and other help first-year teachers need to be successful. Success in the first year or two of teaching is essential to build confidence in teachers and convince them to continue in the profession. Investing in support for new teachers is cost-effective because fewer positions are vacated, thus saving resources otherwise spent on recruiting, hiring, assigning, and inducting new teachers.

Support for new principals is essential as well. Every new principal in BPS, for example, participates in an early summer weeklong program with accomplished principals, central office staff, and local university professors. The focus is on leadership and management. During their first and second years as principals, they participate in a monthly principals' group, which is facilitated by several school district or university educators who have served in school and school district leadership roles. They help them reflect on the challenges of leadership and management and on how to resolve difficult problems and be successful with time management. Each new principal is also mentored during the year by a successful, experienced colleague principal. After principals complete their second year, they often decide to take responsibility for continuing the periodic meetings of the group; this is an important step for leaders to take because of the importance of continuous learning and of modeling what they are learning for those they are leading.

Teacher and Leader Retention

The challenge of turnover is usually focused on teachers because they represent the major employment group in every school district and school. The turnover is highest for teachers in urban school districts; as noted elsewhere, it is typically more than 30 percent in the first three years and 50 percent or more in five years. Suburban and rural districts are not immune to turnover, but the rates are lower. There are many reasons for turnover: lack of success; insufficient support during the first year or more of teaching; poor preparation; discontent with the school culture resulting from few opportunities for collaboration and collegial work; ineffective leadership on the part of the principal; inadequate supplies, materials, and equipment; poor classroom management; nights and weekends spent in planning lessons; pressure to focus on tests and scores; the isolation of the classroom; dissatisfaction with compensation and benefits; and discovery of a bad fit.

In the past, many were attracted to teaching because they saw it as a career that provided security; a defined work day and year; a salary schedule that provided additional pay for staying another year, and the opportunity to increase compensation by taking additional courses or earning a master's degree; defined pension plans; and ample vacations, including a free summer. Those who were interested in moving to another community for a job could do so and be in the same retirement system as long as they stayed in the same state. In the past, most who decided to make teaching a career stayed in one school district, and many remained at the same school. The guaranteed retirement became an incentive to stay put.

In recent decades, the employment options, particularly for women and people of color, have expanded, and no longer are teaching, nursing, or social work the major career options for these groups. During the same time frame, organizations that have developed different ways of thinking about human capital strategies (for example, Teach for America, New Leaders for New Schools, the New Teacher Project, charter schools, and charter management organizations) have stimulated innovations in education. These organizations have been successful in attracting college graduates to teaching and leadership opportunities in education. Their innovative and entrepreneurial approaches, which offer the opportunity to create schools and cultures that are different from mainstream public schools, have been attractive to college graduates who want to try teaching and leading in public schools, but only if they are organized in ways that conform to these students' expectations about collaboration in the workplace and about achievement and accountability for adults as well as students; preference for working in teams rather than in the isolation of the classroom; desire for opportunities for advancement to leadership roles that draw on the learning from innovative leadership and management in other sectors, which challenge some of the thinking about leadership roles in education; interest in setting policy, shaping the nexus where policy and practice align; and attitudes that welcome change and do not see risk as adverse. They also believe that they will change jobs a number of times and perhaps even change careers once or twice.

These changes alone will not resolve the traditional challenges of turnover and lead to greater retention, but they will require a different way of thinking about human capital and how to attract this new generation of college graduates to education. One compelling incentive is the interest many have in social justice issues and their desire to work in a sector where they can make a positive difference.

School and district leaders must also be thinking about other strategies for dealing with the challenges of turnover and retention. Midcareer changes are increasing in all sectors—private, military, nonprofit, and government. These changes create another pool of potential teachers and leaders in public education. Innovative thinking and changes in certification policy, preparation programs, and induction programs will be necessary. Baby boomers are beginning to retire and will be a significant source of adult talent that is interested in schools and could be an enormous asset, not just as volunteers who could make a tremendous difference in filling part-time roles in schools, but as teachers and leaders. Technology must become a major focus of rethinking the way in which people access learning. Virtual schools and classrooms will of necessity become a strategy for addressing the challenges of turnover.

Conclusion

Several centuries ago, Mark Hopkins, the president of Williams College, described education as the teacher on one end of a log and the student on the other. Each must connect with the other to balance the log and ensure effective teaching and learning. There has been an understanding for centuries that the quality of teaching is the essential factor for student learning and that a positive reciprocal relationship between teachers and students is essential. The log analogy may seem difficult to understand in the twenty-first century. There are now many different ways of thinking about teaching and learning, but however we define them now and in the future, what we will do must remain grounded in our developing knowledge and understanding of the importance of the quality of instruction and leadership. Human capital is at the core. We must continue to learn about different ways to develop and use it in ways that serve all students well.

5

Urban School Leadership Skills

A t the core of standards-based reform was the radical idea that all students must meet the rigorous learning standards that traditionally had been the goal for the select groups of students who were expected to graduate from high school ready for some type of postsecondary education. No longer does a high school diploma provide the ticket to a job with decent wages and benefits, nor does it provide the opportunity to acquire middle-class status. For urban district and school leaders, the challenge is to ensure that all students graduate from high school ready— without remediation—for some type of postsecondary education. Reaching this goal requires superintendents and other central office and school administrators to develop the leadership skills necessary to meet this challenge. Traditionally district and school administrators have been trained to be effective managers skillful in executing all the operations that are necessary to keep districts and schools running smoothly. Superintendents, other central office staff, and principals also must acquire the skills to become instructional leaders. They must focus their efforts on improving teaching and student learning and be accountable for the results.

The Risk of Stagnation and the Need for Change

The conflict between keeping things the same and the movement toward change commonly observed in school districts and schools often affects the way educators view their leadership roles. It is tempting to do what we have always done because we are comfortable with the routine and we think it works; change is viewed as a threat to the status quo and to our status as professional leaders, but this can lead to stagnation. School leaders' opinions often are bolstered by anecdotal evidence rather than informed by quantitative and qualitative data. Too often students are blamed for poor achievement results and are held accountable for their own improved performance; rather, this responsibility should be embraced by the leaders and other adults in school districts, schools, and classrooms.

There is a competing focus on change, which is shown when a program, curriculum, or approach does not result in acceptable student performance and the next "obvious" step is to change the curriculum, materials, or assessments. Little thought is given to whether the curriculum is aligned with standards and assessments or if sufficient training is provided to build the capacity of leaders and teachers to implement programs with fidelity. The tension between these conflicting points of view is now increased by the expectation that districts and schools will align curriculum with state standards and enable all students to reach proficiency on state assessments.

The demands of accountability and the transparency of public access to state, district, school, and even classroom student achievement data have changed expectations for what successful leaders need to know and be able to do. Decision making regarding student performance in districts and schools uses data disaggregated by gender, race, socioeconomic standing, disability, and language. The data expose gaps in achievement within these categories and the trajectory of progress toward proficiency. Leaders in school districts and schools are expected to understand data and how to use that information for decision making without enough attention being paid to the reliability and validity of the data. Moreover, when accountability systems ignore the qualitative aspects of teaching and leading, it is unlikely that good decisions will be made from an understanding of what is working and should be sustained and what is not working and requires change.

An effective strategy for new superintendents and principals to assess what should be sustained or changed is to develop an entry plan for their first hundred days. For example, the superintendent's plan should include the following:

- One or two school visits each day.

- A facilitated retreat with the school board to discuss board-superintendent relationships, roles, responsibilities, and communication protocols.

- Meetings with stakeholder groups in the community.

- Individual meetings with central office senior leadership team members.

- Group meetings with gatherings of district staff in the central office and other locations.

- Meetings with union leaders, newspaper and other media editorial boards, presidents of local colleges and universities, deans of schools of education, school principals, business leaders, faith-based leaders, and the mayor and other elected city officials. The superintendent should be prepared to make a brief presentation to each group describing core values and beliefs.

New principals and other school leaders should perform an in-depth review of the existing school improvement plan and of student achievement and other information; they should also reach out to the community. Their stakeholder group will be smaller and easier to define. They should spend extensive time in individual conversations with faculty, staff, and students and also in small- and large-group settings. Their individual classroom visits should focus on the quality of instruction, the composition and role of the school leadership team if one exists, and an assessment of the capacity of the staff. Outreach to parents with a plan for family and community engagement is essential. Principals should also find out what autonomy they have to make decisions at the school sites and what decisions are required to be made by their supervisors or others in the central office.

The information gathered during the first hundred days is essential to developing and implementing a district strategic plan for meeting the goals established by the board and superintendent and by the superintendent and the principals. District and school leaders must seize the opportunity to develop road maps and use the political capital that is usually granted to new leaders to acknowledge what strategies seem to be working and should be sustained and to push the agenda for necessary change to generate improvement.

The following two examples from when I was superintendent of Boston Public Schools (BPS) illustrate the conflict between maintaining the status quo and moving toward change. They highlight the importance of context and the challenge of understanding what the ideal pace of change should be to reach the desired results of improved student achievement. The first example focuses on literacy curriculum and instruction. The second focuses on mathematics curriculum and instruction.

My initial plan involved the creation of a transition team that I appointed with the advice and counsel of key leaders whom I met during the superintendent search and several people I knew at the Harvard Graduate School of Education. The team had only five weeks to prepare a report that included its assessment of BPS and recommendations for the most important issues for me to address during my first year as superintendent.

Improving literacy was high on the list. Performance was at best flat in most schools, and achievement gaps were significant based on data disaggregated by race, disability, language, and free and reduced-price lunch status. There were many different literacy programs in the elementary schools. The first step was to develop citywide learning standards in literacy that aligned with the state's curriculum frameworks. The second step was to determine what type of reading and writing programs would be appropriate to reach those goals. We selected a balanced literacy model and Readers and Writers Workshop for the pedagogy. (Funds were insufficient to cover the costs of a districtwide rollout in a single year. It took several years to implement the new program in all schools.) The third step was to select the first cohort of schools to adopt the new literacy program. Elementary principals were invited to submit proposals for including their schools in the first cohort and describing the approaches they would take and commitments they would make to build the capacity of the staff to implement the new literacy programs. The intended purpose was to determine which principals were ready to take on the new leadership challenge and were able to describe how they would lead and work with their teachers to select and implement one of the literacy programs. This strategy resulted in more than fifty elementary school principals submitting proposals to become one of the thirty-five schools in the first cohort. The process was effective in identifying the principals who were eager for innovation and change, and many of the schools in this first cohort were effective in selecting and implementing the programs and pedagogy.

The rollout of the balanced literacy program continued with the remaining three cohorts in years two, three, and four. The unanticipated outcome was that the schools with the weakest leadership, lowest teacher capacity, and lowest student achievement did not take the initiative to join the second- or third-year cohorts. They waited until year four to make the change. As superintendent I learned an important lesson about delegating important decision making. The schools in the first cohort showed the capacity and commitment of their school leaders and staff. However, the schools with the weakest student achievement results and capacity to improve should not have been given the leeway to wait and be last to adopt the new balanced literacy program.

This experience helped me think more clearly about centralized and decentralized decision making. Should school district leaders allow schools to make decisions based only on evidence of their capacity and commitment to do so? Or should schools be encouraged or perhaps forced to embrace changes that better address the needs of the students? These are not easy questions to answer. However, with the benefit of hindsight, I would not have second-guessed the strategy used with the first cohort, but I would have required the lowest-performing schools to join the second cohort to raise student achievement in an environment where resources were insufficient to fund a districtwide change strategy in a single year or two.

The change strategy for improving mathematics was different. The decision had been made to select a districtwide curriculum for elementary, K–8, middle, and high schools. Resources were available to provide training for teachers and to roll out the program at all levels simultaneously. The selection of TERC Investigations for elementary grades, Connected Math for middle grades, and Math Connections for high schools was bold because of the extensive training teachers needed to implement the program. It was clear early on that the Math Connections program did not align well with the traditional Algebra I, Geometry, Algebra II, Pre-Calculus, and Calculus sequence in high schools. Modifications were made to support this sequence when BPS decided to set new district requirements for high school graduation that included four years of mathematics and passing Algebra II as well as three years of lab science—biology, chemistry, and physics.

The key lessons I learned when improving literacy in BPS did challenge conventional practice about how fast or slow change should be implemented. During the first three years of implementing the new math curriculum in elementary, K–8, and middle schools, achievement results on the state mathematics test were flat at best. In the fourth year, the gains were modest, and from 2004 through 2009 the gains were steady. BPS was one of the urban school districts that volunteered to participate in the National Assessment of Educational Progress (NAEP) Urban

Trials in which fourth- and eighth-grade results in literacy and mathematics were reported for fifteen large urban school districts. The results for Boston's fourth- and eighth-grade students have improved each year and consistently have been in the top quartile of the participating urban districts. In 2004, Boston's gains in mathematics on the fourth- and eighth-grade NAEP were the largest one-year gain that the NAEP staff had seen in an urban school district. The gains have continued to increase, judging from 2006 and 2008 fourth- and eighth-grade results.

During the first three years of flat results, there was a lot of pressure from the teachers union and some other groups to change the math curriculum. The investment made in the purchase of materials and training of teachers as well as the challenge of cutting $85 million from the school district's budget during the 2003–04 fiscal year made it easier politically to stay the course. It also was a powerful lesson learned that it is essential to invest time and resources to create deep understanding of how to define a strategy, build the capacity of the teachers and school leaders to execute it with fidelity, and show the results of improved student achievement to scale.

Empowering People

Successful leaders understand that they are powerless if they do not engage the people they lead in collaborating to achieve specific results. Often leaders have great flexibility to decide whether the people in the existing organization have the right skill set and commitment to take the organization to the next level of performance. They retain those who embrace the leader's vision and demonstrate the will and skill to do the necessary work to achieve positive results. Thoughtful new leaders don't assume that they can succeed only by starting over. They look for those in the organization who have talent but have not been given the opportunity to stretch their abilities, offer alternative strategies for reaching goals, and respond to incentives that challenge the status quo or address the dysfunctional aspects of the organizational structure. Successful leaders seek the appropriate balance between finding and developing people within the organization and recruiting effective people from outside the organization.

There is less flexibility in urban public school districts and schools. New principals inherit a teaching staff with a significant number of tenured teachers. They have to wait for vacancies before they are able to pick their own staff. In many schools they have little flexibility because teachers with transfer rights are entitled to fill openings in their schools, or teachers who are shifted from other schools must be placed somewhere by the central office. Superintendents may have more flexibility and include in their contract the right to select a senior leadership team or fill other vacant positions. In many districts, however, administrators are secure in their positions, and only a few serve at the will of the superintendent. Most will recruit and select some people from outside the district to serve on their senior leadership teams.

Creating instructional leadership teams is an effective strategy to empower teachers and other staff selected by the principal to develop the school's improvement plan. It is important for the school district to develop a framework for a whole-school improvement plan. The plans are designed to be living documents with annual review and revisions. The BPS framework has seven essentials:

The Seven Essentials of Whole-School Improvement

The Core Essential: Effective Instruction

Use effective and culturally relevant instructional practices and create a collaborative school climate that improves student learning, promotes student engagement, and builds on prior knowledge and experiences.

Essential Two: Student Work and Data

Examine student work and data to drive instruction and professional development.

Essential Three: Professional Development

Invest in professional development to improve instruction.

Essential Four: Shared Leadership

Share leadership to sustain instructional improvement.

Essential Five: Resources

Focus resources to support instructional improvement and improve student learning.

Essential Six: Families and Community

Partner with families and community to support student learning and engagement.

Essential Seven: Operational Excellence

Maintain high levels of effectiveness, efficiency, and equity in operations.

The core essential is instruction, and the other six essentials are aligned to serve the core essential. Shared leadership enables principals to distribute responsibilities and engage other school administrators and teacher-leaders in decision making with the expectation that they also are part of a team that embraces and models accountability for results. When leadership responsibilities are distributed and carried out as intended, school leaders are modeling a process that demonstrates to the rest of the staff the value of transforming school culture from one where teachers are isolated in their classrooms to one of collaboration and shared decision making, which empowers those in different roles to participate in shaping the school improvement plan.

When the plan is completed, the entire team owns it and the principal and the teacher team members share responsibility for getting the rest of the staff to embrace the plan before it is submitted to the school site council for approval. Teachers who work as part of the team to improve student achievement create a sustaining collaborative culture in schools that also engages and empowers the rest of the faculty and school site council as they review, develop, own, and execute their plans for school improvement.

During my first six months as superintendent of BPS, I appointed 10 of the 125 principals to a newly created position of cluster leader to empower school leaders and distribute responsibility for leadership across the school district. There were ten clusters of schools defined by geographic regions, each with a mix of 12 to 13 principals from elementary, K–8, middle, and high schools. The cluster leaders continued in their full-time roles as principals. Each month they convened and led a meeting of the principals in their clusters, at which they discussed with their colleagues the issues they were facing. Time also was designated at each meeting to focus on a problem of practice identified by the group during the previous month. This enabled the cluster leader to invite district staff members who would provide appropriate premeeting materials and join the group at its next meeting.

Principals were also able to contact their cluster leaders at any time for advice and support. The cluster leaders were members of my expanded leadership team, which met twice a month. They also participated in the development of the school district budget with the senior leadership team. They receive additional compensation for this role and were empowered to bring their expertise to the discussion of district issues through their continuous engagement with my expanded leadership team. The key lesson learned was that before final decisions are made, it is important to engage at the outset those who are charged with the responsibility for implementing programs in schools and classrooms in the discussion of what support is necessary to achieve the intended results. Neglecting this reality check can lead to unintended consequences.

Another strategy for empowering educators and parents was the creation of pilot schools in BPS. School legislation in Massachusetts authorizes the Massachusetts State Board of Education to approve applications for charter schools. Prior to 2010, local school districts could not approve charter schools. They are responsible for allocating funds for their students who enroll in independent charter schools approved by the state. In 1994 the Boston Teachers Union and BPS agreed to open several pilot schools that were designed to have most of the autonomies granted to the state-approved charters. The major difference was the requirement for a joint labor management committee cochaired by the superintendent and teachers union president to sign off on proposals for pilot schools before the proposals could be considered and approved by the Boston School Committee, which was the governing board for BPS. Between 1994 and 2009, twenty-two pilot schools were opened within BPS, and the model has been adopted in several other states where in-district charter schools authorized by local school boards are not an option. The pilot schools provide a model for empowering educators, parents, and communities to design innovative schools that provide additional options for educators, teachers unions, parents, and school boards in school districts that adopt policies to support school choice.

Common Leadership Roles

The size of school districts and schools is a major factor in determining the number and types of leadership roles. There are still a few school districts with a single school, where the leader serves as the superintendent of the district, as the principal of the school, and as a teacher as well. And then there is New York City, with more than a million students, hundreds of schools, thousands of teachers, hundreds of principals and other administrators, and a chancellor, appointed by the mayor and his appointed board, who has the duties of a superintendent. Context is important and does result in some differentiation in leadership roles and responsibilities. This section focuses on the common roles and responsibilities of leaders in school districts and schools. It also reinforces our understanding of how resources are allocated in school districts in which on average 80 percent of the budget covers salaries and benefits and in schools in which the amount is 90 to 95 percent. In my experience personnel decisions are the most important decisions leaders make.

A district's organization chart should provide a visual representation of the way the district is organized, the titles of key positions, and the reporting relationships. The school board typically is at the top of the chart with the superintendent as a direct report. Some districts contract with outside legal counsel. Often larger districts hire in-house counsel. Most districts use a bidding process to select outside firms to conduct annual financial audits. In districts with legal counsel and auditors, the reporting line may be to the board and the superintendent.

Often tensions in school districts are created by disparate views on how many and which positions report to the superintendent and what the titles should be. It is difficult to generalize roles based on their titles. For example, in very small districts, the principals may report directly to the superintendent. The business manager, who often is responsible for the budget, payroll, maintenance, and other operations, is another direct report. The superintendent may have a curriculum specialist to help the schools improve teaching and learning. Even in small districts, common roles and responsibilities are defined by operational functions and curriculum and instruction functions. In larger districts, the tendency is to differentiate and refine responsibilities within those areas. However, different titles may have similar roles. In a few large districts, the leader in the superintendent's role may be called a *chief education officer, chief executive officer,* or *chancellor.* Direct reports may include positions with titles such as *deputy superintendent, associate superintendent, assistant superintendent, chief academic officer, chief operating officer, chief financial officer,* or other titles beginning with *chief*. Again context and past practice are important to understand when district leaders determine who their direct reports will be and whether only direct reports will be members of the senior leadership team.

Creating an appropriate organization chart is complicated. As discussed previously, it is wise for a new superintendent first to spend several months listening and learning, visiting schools, engaging stakeholders, determining the strengths and weaknesses of current central office staff, reviewing data, and conducting audits. One approach is to design the organization to align with the mission of the school district's strategic plan to improve achievement for all students. This construct supports crossfunctionality among departments as well as shared accountability for results. However, no organization will succeed without having people with the appropriate skills in the right positions to lead the work. Some of the inherited staff serving in current central office positions might not have the necessary leadership skills to be effective in the roles defined by the reorganization. The challenge becomes to identify and assign the people with the skills required to succeed.

Another approach is for a new superintendent to use the information gleaned from listening and learning during the first three months to determine the level of current leadership talent already in place. With this information it is possible to determine how the organization chart should be changed to align with the existing talent. If resources are available, a third approach is to have an organizational audit done by an outside contractor who specializes in this area. This approach provides more time for the superintendent to assess the skills of the current district leaders and benefit from the advice of an outside expert before making final decisions about what the key district leadership roles should be and who should fill them.

The Chief Academic Officer

Ten years ago, it would have been difficult for me to predict that by 2010 the chief academic officer would become a common anchor position on the senior leadership teams in many school districts. Two different position descriptions have evolved for this role. One is similar to the position description developed in the past for the roles of deputy associate or assistant superintendent for teaching and learning or curriculum and instruction. The span of control generally covered central office leaders of curriculum development, professional development, special education, gifted and talented education, English language learner education, and other similar programs. The title *chief academic officer* has become more common for senior leadership team members with these responsibilities. Districts using this description have other titles for those who supervise school principals—for example, *area, regional, deputy, associate,* and *assistant superintendents.*

The chief academic officer role also often includes oversight of those who supervise the principals in the schools. The span of control is enormous and typically requires the chief academic officer in a large district to have ten or more direct reports. The superintendent will be two to three levels removed from the principals in this school district structure. Certainly the size of the school district is an important variable in determining the amount of contact the superintendent has with principals. Knowing that the quality of leadership in schools is second only to the quality of instruction in classrooms, superintendents, regardless of their district size, should be intentional about connecting with principals. My own practice as a superintendent was to have no more than one level between me and the principals. In Boston I had three deputies who supervised and evaluated principals. I reviewed each evaluation, discussed them with the deputies, and signed them personally. Each year I conducted three or four evaluations myself. This practice sent a strong message to principals about my connection with their leadership roles and the importance of the work they do.

Here are some strategies for how to connect with principals:

- Join the supervisor of the principal for the final interview of the candidate recommended before signing off on the appointment.

- Make unannounced visits to schools a priority early in the day with the goal of visiting at least three schools each week.

- Spend some time at the beginning of the visit with the principal one-on-one and ask for a brief update on the implementation of the school improvement plan and any data the principal has to share. Depending on the size of the school, leave forty-five minutes or more to visit some classrooms with the principal and share comments about your observations as you move from class to class.

- Consider having principal representation at your leadership team meetings.

- Participate in the districtwide professional development required for principals.

- Arrange to join the immediate supervisors of the principals in discussions about their evaluations.

- Serve as an evaluator of two or three principals each year.

- Appoint successful principals to serve as cluster leaders and bring small groups of principals together from a cluster of ten to twelve schools each month to discuss issues they are facing and how they are resolving them. Include the cluster leaders in meetings of an expanded leadership team and reward them with extra compensation.

- Schedule two-hour meetings with all principals three times a year and dedicate an hour to an hour and a half to professional development of their leadership skills. Allow thirty minutes for principals to ask questions of the superintendent, which will be answered by the superintendent with the help of other senior staff as necessary.

- Meet monthly during the school year with the leaders of the principals' organization.

Teacher-Leader Roles

The focus of this section has been on the common roles of leaders at the central office and in schools. New roles are emerging for teacher-leaders as well. Instructional leadership teams in schools provide the opportunity for teachers to become part of the school team that develops the whole school improvement plan and works with their colleagues to embrace and implement it. Other teacher leadership opportunities might include positions as coaches, staff developers, curriculum coordinators, accreditation team members, district committee members or chairs, and leadership roles on school site councils, in teachers unions and professional organizations, and as mentors for new teachers.

These teacher leadership roles are for those who want to stay in classrooms and teach but also want to develop their leadership skills and contribute to school improvement efforts and enhance their compensation. Others will aspire to leadership roles and become future administrators in schools and school districts.

Difficult Speeches

At the beginning of each school year I prepared and delivered an address to all employees in the school district. The purpose was to acknowledge the importance of the work of *all* district employees, not just teachers, principals, and other educators. Too often the employees who work in the central office and schools are not acknowledged for the important support they provide to those who focus on teaching and learning and have daily contact with students in schools and classrooms. My goal was to acknowledge the accomplishments of the previous year, set high expectations for continuous improvement during the new school year, and clarify the two or three most important strategies we would use to achieve our goals. These speeches were difficult to construct because my self-imposed commitment was to take no more than fifteen to twenty minutes to deliver my remarks.

In August 1969, I became superintendent of Springfield Township, a suburban Philadelphia school district that had eight schools and forty-five hundred students. I gave my first speech to all employees, convened with room to spare, in the junior high school auditorium. I read my speech, which is difficult to do well in the best of circumstances, and it took longer than I had anticipated. The audience was gracious and I learned that less is more if the message is crisp, clear, focused, and relevant. My beginning-of-school speeches during the next three years were more focused, shorter, and each delivered from an outline of the prepared text that was printed and available for all after I delivered it.

During my five years as superintendent in Eugene, Oregon, a district with twenty-two thousand students and fifteen hundred employees, I chose the largest high school auditorium for my address. With the backing of the school board that hired me, I addressed two controversial issues that created divisions in the community and that led to the election of several new board members who promised to hire a new superintendent. The first issue was to provide public kindergarten programs in every elementary school. The school district budget had to be approved annually by the public. For years there had been an additional item on the ballot that required voters to decide whether or not to fund public kindergartens; it had never been approved. My recommendation to include the cost of the program in the school district budget was viewed as an inappropriate action that removed the public's right to vote on the issue. My argument then and always has been that a school district budget should be the financial plan to support the implementation of the education plan, which includes programs that will guarantee quality education for all children. Kindergarten for all Eugene children had to be available in Eugene's public schools. It was an equity issue. For years parents who could afford kindergarten tuition were able to send their children to programs offered by the private providers who leased space in Eugene elementary schools. Although I was not permitted to advocate the ballot measure, I could as an educator talk about the benefits of early childhood education and the importance of all children having access to it. Staying on the right side of the line in my stump speeches—for example, providing information to voters about a local ballot measure to pass a school district budget, approve a bond issue to cover the costs of building new schools, or approve a tax increase to support the school district's operating budget—was appropriate. In contrast, advocacy for getting people to the polls and suggesting how they should vote was not. Three elections were held to gain approval of the school district budget. It was defeated twice. The third time was the charm. By a margin of thirteen votes with thousands of votes cast, followed by a recount and court challenge, the budget that included the resources for publicly funded kindergartens passed. The political consequences were substantial. For many who voted against the kindergarten measure, the real issue was that of eliminating their right to vote on a specific program. The school board and I had taken away the public's right to vote on the kindergarten issue by including the program in the district budget.

The second controversy, which created dramatic splits in the community, was the result of my decision—supported by a majority of the school board members—to move three of the four high school principals in the district to three junior high schools and replace them with the three junior high school principals. The reassigned high school principals retained their salaries but argued that their status had been damaged. The short speech that I made in presenting the recommendation to the school board was difficult. It had to be nuanced and was grounded in my belief that both schools and leaders can benefit from periodic changes in leadership. The high schools were adept at maintaining the status quo and eschewing change. The three junior high principals were eager to accept the leadership challenge of balancing what should be sustained and what should be changed in the high schools and also wanted to be accountable for the results. What followed was one of the toughest school board meetings of my career, held in a school gymnasium with six hundred people, most of whom were opposed to my reassignments of the principals. The purpose of the meeting was to hear public comment; it lasted more than three hours. Before the meeting concluded, I was given the opportunity to respond. Listening to several hours of attacks, many of them personal, is difficult for any leader. Responding defensively or emotionally in that context would have fueled the anger expressed by many of the speakers. I used my five minutes to state why I reassigned the principals, which in my opinion was in the best interest of the students in the schools. I spoke extemporaneously. However, I had carefully prepared my remarks, which I used when the school board approved my recommendation and during my conversations with the press. The challenge was to be clear about the reasons for the reassignments without crossing the line and discussing individual personal matters that weren't appropriate for the public to hear.

A final example of a difficult speech to give is a eulogy when someone in the school community dies. When I was superintendent of Oklahoma City Public Schools, it was my practice to listen to news radio when in the car. As I was returning to the office from a Rotary luncheon, I heard a news flash reporting an explosion at one of our elementary schools. No details were available. The office was only a few blocks away, and as soon as I arrived I was told the name of the school, that there had been an explosion, that an unknown number of students and adults were injured, and that those with the most serious injuries were being taken by helicopter to local hospitals. Television, radio, and print media people were already on the scene and were looking for a spokesperson to interview. No central office leaders were as yet at the school. During the twenty-minute drive, news radio kept reporting fresh and increasingly disheartening information every few minutes as I was struggling to get my thoughts together about what I would say when I had few details about what had happened. This was before cell phones, and I did not have a car phone. I knew that what I would say and how I would say it would be seen and heard by more people than anything I had done in the past.

When I arrived at the school, ambulances were still taking children and adults to hospitals. The press had been assigned a designated area on the school playground to set up cameras and conduct interviews. By this time district maintenance personnel were present, and I learned from them that a water heater in a small room adjacent to the school cafeteria had exploded during the lunch period. There were no answers yet that I could give to questions seeking details on what happened and why. My first of what would be dozens of interviews during the next week to ten days left the press frustrated because my focus was on the students and adults who were injured and the support being provided by a number of city and county agencies who were collaborating, following rapid response emergency plans and protocols, and saving lives. The demand for blood at local hospitals was high, and by early evening lines of volunteers ready to donate blood had formed at city and area hospitals where the injured were being treated. Many were in critical condition. Fortunately most survived and recovered in time. The tragedy was the death of five children and a teacher.

During the next few days, I personally visited the homes of the deceased, and five of the six families welcomed my visit. One family screamed at me when they opened the door and ordered me to leave their property. I was asked by the five families to attend the funerals, and one family asked me to speak, which I did. Acknowledgment of the pain we all experience with the death of a loved one, celebration of the life of the deceased, and respect for the religion of the deceased's family are what district and school leaders must provide when they are asked to make remarks or deliver a eulogy.

Leaders must understand that there are many unanticipated events that affect the lives of those they lead and their own lives as well. In those situations, often there is no forewarning and time to think and reflect on how to respond and what to say. Developing the skill of knowing what to do when there is not the luxury of gathering more data, seeking the advice of others, or having ample time for contemplation is important and can be learned by studying how others approach this challenge and reflecting on what has and has not been effective.

Tough Decisions

The previous section focused on making difficult speeches. They often go hand in hand with making tough decisions. I have emphasized the critical leadership skill of gathering the right personnel and placing the right people in positions that align with their skills. Developing the capacity to help employees acquire new skills and enable them to take on more demanding leadership roles in districts and schools is also essential. These and other skills were the focus in Chapter Four, where the emphasis was on developing human capital and leadership in managing people. Tough decisions are made when employees are hired, assigned, evaluated, promoted, and terminated.

In the private and nonprofit sectors, leaders often serve at will or have fixed-term contracts. Typically leaders have annual performance goals, and their evaluation is based on achievement of those goals. Compensation also is based on performance. In the public education sector, states require school and school district leaders to meet certification requirements to serve in leadership positions. Superintendents in most states have fixed-term contracts issued by school boards that vary in length from one to five years. Increasingly these contracts include annual performance goals and an evaluation process.

Some direct reports to the superintendent in a large district also may have fixed-term contracts. Other district leaders may serve at the will of the superintendent but have the ability to fall back to a different administrative or teaching position in the schools if they have the proper state certification. In a few states, principals serve on fixed-term contracts. In others, school leaders can acquire tenure, or collective bargaining contracts provide them with other job protection rights. Context is very important in determining the degree of flexibility school leaders have to make hiring and termination decisions.

Deciding to terminate employees and taking the necessary and appropriate action to do so are difficult in any sector. The field of employment law has expanded dramatically in recent years. District and school leaders must meet tougher requirements and follow due process to justify termination. The evaluation of employees is time-consuming and requires adherence to state statutes, the school district's evaluation policies, and, if they exist, local collective bargaining agreements.

Hiring is the first tough decision point for district and school leaders, and the second is deciding who to retain when the probationary period ends. The best practice is for leaders who are held accountable for evaluating their staff to participate in and ideally make initial hiring decisions and determine who should be retained at the end of the probationary period. It is particularly tough when there are not a sufficient number of applicants in the hard-to-fill fields, and district and school leaders must open the school year with a teacher in every classroom. This may affect how leaders make decisions about continuing the employment of those who are at the end of their probationary years. Managing multiple responsibilities pulls leaders in many directions, and too often it becomes a problem of time management when the most important and often time-intensive tasks, such as evaluation of employees, are not given the priority necessary to make the tough personnel decisions. The superintendent must model the behavior for those in leadership positions and set clear expectations for selecting, supporting, evaluating, and continuing or terminating employees.

Superintendents face tough decisions when they make policy, personnel, budget, and other recommendations that school boards must approve. When there is a clear understanding about roles and responsibilities and good communication between the board and the superintendent, and they take responsibility together for tough decisions, it is easier to address any controversy that may arise.

The following are additional examples of some tough decisions and difficult speeches I have made as a superintendent.

Closing Schools

There are many examples of what criteria to use to develop recommendations to school boards for school closure, including demographic and enrollment data, condition of school buildings, cost of keeping schools open and savings with proposed school closures, alternative uses of vacated facilities, equitable distribution of school closures in areas of the school district, achievement data, and student and staff reassignment plans. Process is very important. One option is to have school staff develop the plan and schedule meetings in the regions of the school district where school closures are proposed to explain the plan and allow community members to have an opportunity to comment while the superintendent and several board members are also in attendance. Following the community meetings, the staff and superintendent can then make modifications to the plan prior to submitting it to the school board for approval. Even when this process is used, and despite the power of data that show that a school is underachieving, losing enrollment, and too costly to operate, families with children in the school turn out at community and school board meetings arguing that the school should be saved because it is one of the very best in the district. Their sincere intent is to use the power of emotion to trump the logic of data and the need to reallocate limited resources to best serve the needs of all students. In my experience, it is very difficult to approach school closures one school at a time unless there are major safety issues or other compelling reasons. Presenting a thoughtful plan for closing a group of schools, rather than recommending individual school closures over several years, consolidates the tough decisions.

Changing School Attendance Boundaries

Expanding and shrinking school district enrollment as well as addressing issues of race and class are often critical variables that drive changes in school attendance boundaries. In recent years the courts have continued to restrict the use of race as a variable in deciding school attendance boundaries. Some districts are still using socioeconomic (class) data as a variable for defining school attendance areas. As noted previously, declining school enrollment is a major reason for closing schools, and therefore boundary changes are often necessary. When a community builds new homes that house school-age children, either schools must be built and new school attendance areas established or students will have to be transported to other schools that have available space. The politics of these changes are difficult, particularly for families who have purchased or leased homes in an area to ensure attendance at a particular school.

School choice is one way to mitigate the tough decisions and problems associated with boundary changes. School choice relies heavily on lottery systems, which work well for families who get their choices, but not for those who are dissatisfied with the choices they receive. (They may decide to leave the public schools if they can afford to do so.) Equity issues are involved as well.

To ensure equal access, transportation must be provided for students whose families are not able to transport them to the schools they have chosen. One positive outcome of a choice system is the motivation it generates for schools to improve—an essential ingredient for attracting students. It challenges the complacency of those who have the attitude that we are doing fine and that if we just open our doors, new students will enroll.

Resource Allocation

Tough decisions have to be made at the classroom, school, district, state, and federal levels in good times and bad times. I can't think of any year in my thirty-seven as superintendent that the school district budget as finally adopted had sufficient resources to meet the needs of all students. Although district and school leaders must be strong advocates for additional resources, they cannot use the lack of resources as an excuse for low performance. Once the budget is approved, leaders must still set high expectations for leveraging the resources available to provide value added as defined by improved achievement for all students. The message should be that we will do the best we can with the resources we have, and we will make resource allocation decisions based on evidence from programs yielding positive results. It is difficult to avoid cutting positions to balance budgets when most districts, regardless of size, have 80 percent of their budget allocated to salaries and benefits. Understandably the first priority is to hold the schools harmless and cut positions in the district offices. However, the significant cuts brought on by the deep recession beginning in the 2007–08 school year are continuing in 2010 to force states and school districts to make deeper cuts, which have been mitigated to some extent by federal stimulus funds.

School Board–Superintendent Relationships

When relationships between the superintendent and the school board are good, other district leaders in the central office and schools are able to fulfill their leadership responsibilities with clarity about district priorities. If there is dissonance within the board or between the board and the superintendent, other district leaders are not absolved of their responsibility to stay focused on teaching and learning and ensure that the work of the district continues. Superintendents are responsible for bringing recommendations to the school board. If the board approves all recommendations, the board may be accused of being a "rubber stamp" for the superintendent, which over time can erode the public's confidence in them both. Building and sustaining positive relationships between the board and superintendent are joint responsibilities.

Most states allow school boards to discuss personnel decisions in executive sessions. Difficult situations often result when individual board members or several board members challenge the superintendent's recommendations for the appointment of principals or district leaders and have their own candidates for the positions. The tough decision for the superintendent is how to respond. If a majority of the board is opposed to the recommendation, the superintendent has to decide whether to force the board to decide in a public session, which might result in a rejection of the recommendation and a withdrawal of the recommendation in executive sessions. The superintendent will need to consider other potential candidates to recommend to the board at a future meeting after discussing options with the board president at the next agenda planning meeting. It is important for the superintendent to acknowledge the concerns about personnel appointments raised by individual board members. However, the superintendent must remind the board that the accountability for the evaluation and performance of the staff rests with the superintendent and that the board will hold the superintendent responsible for doing so. If individual board members step outside their roles and insist on the appointment of their candidates for leadership roles in the school district and they are not successful, the accountability for the performance of those appointees will still rest with the superintendent.

In San Diego, there was a board member who was upset with the performance of a principal who I believed was performing well in a school with many challenges and a staff that was resistant to change. The board member, without my knowledge, contacted the teachers union building representatives at the school with the request to convene an after-school meeting with all the teachers, at which he would preside and listen to concerns. The board member attended the meeting and distributed ballots to the staff to vote yes or no on a no-confidence resolution and removal of the principal. The results were tallied; a significant majority supported the no-confidence resolution. The press had the story and my tough decision was whether or not to address the inappropriate behavior in public. I discussed the options with the president of the school board and took the position that it would be irresponsible for me to allow one of our school leaders to be treated in such a harsh and inappropriate way. I commented to the press, and a few days later at the next school board meeting, I gave my superintendent's report at the beginning of the meeting with a statement about the inappropriate behavior of the board member, who was sitting two seats away from me. The board president followed my remarks with her own, which reinforced what I had said. The board voted to reprimand their colleague for his inappropriate behavior.

There was one other time during my career as a superintendent that I faced a similar challenge and confronted a board member for inappropriate behavior. In the eighth month of my first year as superintendent in Oklahoma City, the teachers voted to strike at the beginning of the school year. The school board and I were meeting regularly and, consistent with state law, had the authority to consider collective bargaining matters in executive sessions. One of the board members was a leader in a trade union. In the early stages of the strike, which lasted nine days, the board regularly engaged in phone conversations and executive sessions with me, and district strategies and other information for breaking the strike were discussed. All information was confidential. During the course of the strike, I learned that the board member who worked with the trade union was passing this confidential information to the president of the teachers union.

It was a tough decision to confront him and to do so by going alone and unannounced to his home on a Sunday. He denied the allegations. However, until the strike was over, he was not included in further conversations with the other board members about the district's strategies. At the end of each day for the duration of the strike, the board president and I held a press conference to provide the media with a status report. The board member who had been leaking information to the teachers union received only the information from the media briefing. Several years later, after I left Oklahoma City to serve as superintendent in San Diego, I learned that my former board member was indicted, tried, convicted, and sent to jail for crimes unrelated to his work as a school board member.

This chapter has focused on the leadership skills that urban district and school leaders must develop to be successful. Most of the examples provided from my own experience are transferable, but there will always be some leadership skills that are unique to a particular leader's context. And there always will be unanticipated leadership challenges that leaders could never imagine they would have to confront, and knowing what to do when they don't know is an essential characteristic of leadership in such situations. Chapter Six addresses the challenges the next generation of leaders will face and what they will need to be successful.

6

Challenges Facing the Next Generation
of Urban School Leaders

This chapter addresses the complexities of leading urban schools and school districts. For centuries, the United States has been the destination for immigrants who seek opportunity for a better life. The public schools in urban school districts have educated millions of newcomers to the United States and many other generations of those who have migrated from rural communities to urban school districts. Diversity as defined by race, class, culture, language, and abilities has created both challenges and opportunities for leaders in urban school districts and schools. This chapter describes the challenges in and responsibilities leaders have for educating all students, including special education students and English language learners, to meet high standards and graduate from high school ready without remediation for postsecondary education. Other sections address the following:

- Instructional strategies for improving student achievement and narrowing achievement gaps

- Support for continual learning by teachers and other staff to use differentiated instruction and remain faithful to the implementation of curriculum and programs

- Examples from Boston Public Schools' "seven essentials" framework (outlined in Chapter Five) and how leaders can use it to improve teaching and learning

- Challenges facing central office staff who are leading from the middle
- Advice on how state and federal government policies affect district and school leadership

Race

The United States has struggled with race and class since its beginning. The courts have arbitrated these issues from the time slavery was first challenged. The *Brown* v. *Board of Education* decision in 1954 required and constrained a variety of approaches to desegregating and integrating public schools. Despite the decisions of activist courts since then, resegregation, typically linked to class and the changing demographics in urban and rural America, is recurring in some areas of the country. Access to low-skill jobs and low-cost housing disproportionately affects people of color and often limits options for where they can live and find work. In some suburban communities surrounding major cities, racial diversity has increased because the middle class has migrated from the cities to the suburbs. Many urban centers are still the destination for immigrants and are places where several generations of people, particularly those of color, have been unemployed or stuck in low-wage jobs and low-cost or subsidized public housing. The aspirations for this population, despite cynical views to the contrary, are to help their children find a way out of poverty through education in good schools with caring and effective teachers and school and district leaders.

Conversations about race are difficult to lead, particularly for those who have little or no experience living in racially diverse neighborhoods, attending racially diverse schools, or working in racially diverse settings. Moreover, just being in a diverse setting doesn't necessarily advance understanding of race and class issues without the commitment of leaders to make it a priority. This understanding may take leaders out of their comfort zone. It also requires the willingness of leaders to confront their own bias and acquire the skills to lead the difficult conversations about race and to be honest in how they view the races of others and how they react to how people of other races view them. Throughout this book, I've discussed the responsibility of leaders to focus on all students' achieving at high levels. This means that achievement gaps, which are typically defined by race and class, must be narrowed and ultimately closed. Most urban school districts and schools are attempting to do so.

Where should leaders begin? Superintendents should take responsibility for arranging and leading training for the leaders. They must lead by example, participate in all training sessions, and be very clear about why the training is necessary and what the expectations are for all participants. Even though all district and school leaders are involved in the training, there will be those who are ready to take the lead with their own staff and others who will need additional training. Role playing in mixed-race groups is an important part of the training. For three consecutive years while I was superintendent in Boston, the annual summer institute for district and school leaders focused on developing leadership skills for addressing issues concerning race and class, the narrowing and closing of achievement gaps, and skill development in leading difficult conversations on these issues.

Leaders should first ask their staff why they think there are achievement gaps and why they are often defined by race and class. This may be a difficult conversation to lead. Many will be reluctant to participate because they think they can't be candid. Conversations will have to be continued over time. The issue is complex, views will be diverse, and some will refuse to participate. Others may think that "those kids can't reach the standards we have set for all students." Others will say, "It is our obligation to do what is necessary to enable all students to reach the standards and graduate from high school regardless of race and class." My experience has convinced me that focusing the conversation on trying to change the core beliefs of individuals through continuous debate often reaches a point of deadlock, and it is unlikely that some people's beliefs or behaviors will change. However, high achievement is much harder to refute. In most urban school districts, some teachers have students who are significantly outperforming their peers in other classrooms. These examples present a perfect opportunity to determine what is making the positive difference in the quality of instruction in the high-performing classrooms and schools. Evidence-based data are powerful.

Analysis of Data: Number Crunching

Relatively recently data have become the focus of conversation in school districts and schools. Of course teachers have been providing report cards for students for many generations. School leaders had access to their teachers' report cards, but it was unusual for a school's data to be released for public review. If districts gave annual achievement tests in certain grades, the data would be shared with the schools but not with the public. It used to be rare to hear conversations about accountability that focused on student achievement data and the performance of principals, teachers, and superintendents. What a change with the advent of standards-based reform in the early 1990s. However, the original thinking about data and accountability was that there should be formative assessments for teachers to use to determine the progress students were making during the school year and that end-of-year tests would be used for accountability. Since 2000, the focus on data has increased dramatically. As of this publication, the Obama administration and Secretary of Education Arne Duncan are supporting performance management and compensation based on the performance of teachers and school and district leaders. This is not such a new idea for superintendents and school boards, who in recent years have agreed to performance contracts where gains in student achievement and narrowing of achievement gaps are key indicators.

However, using student achievement data to judge teacher quality and determine compensation is controversial. School districts that have developed pay-for-performance plans tend to be located in right-to-work states and not subject to the constraints that often exist in states with public employee collective bargaining statutes and the frequent strong union opposition to pay for performance. The dominant focus in this current era of accountability has been a narrow spotlight on test results as the major accountability indicator. Lost is the increasing evidence that the quality of instruction in the classroom is the most important variable in the school that affects student achievement, which supports the argument for using qualitative indicators and data in accountability systems. This issue is also addressed in the section on federal and state roles and policies.

Instructional Improvement

Instructional improvement in every urban school district, school, and classroom is a major theme of this book. Becoming an instructional leader in a complex environment requires additional focus on how to meet the needs of all children while recognizing that a one-size-fits-all approach will not work. One of the complexities leaders face is how to determine what is standard and what is unique in teaching students in urban school districts and schools with higher concentrations of English language learners, children with special needs, and dropouts. In order for all students to succeed and graduate from high school, urban district and school leaders must have a strong commitment to embrace equity, which requires that standards will not be lowered for some students. Differentiated instruction will be necessary to provide the support for student learning, and a differentiated allocation of resources is essential to provide equitable access to this learning for all students. In addition to the quality of instruction, the variables of time, differentiated instruction, resource allocation, and fidelity of implementation of curriculum and programs are important. The focus here is on programs that serve students with disabilities, English language learners, gifted and talented students, and dropouts in schools that also serve an array of students without special needs.

Achievement Gaps

The goal of educating each child to graduate from high school with the skills necessary for postsecondary education, a career, and a good life depends on district and school leaders' making the commitment with school boards to narrow and ultimately close the gaps in achievement between white and Asian students and black and Latino students. This is what leaders must do, but the challenge is how to do it. State policy in Massachusetts requires students who graduate from 2003 onward to pass both the English language arts and mathematics portions of the Massachusetts Comprehensive Assessment System (MCAS). When the Boston Public Schools (BPS) class of 2003 took the tests during their tenth-grade year in 2001, only 40 percent passed both tests. The results in other urban districts in the state also created concern that a large percentage of high school seniors, despite opportunities in their junior and senior years to retake the test, would not graduate in 2003. A line was drawn between those who advocated for the legislature to rescind the MCAS-passing requirement and those who wanted local school districts to determine their own course completion requirements. A few urban district superintendents, some members of urban school committees (school boards in Massachusetts), and a racially diverse group of community leaders challenged those who were pressing the legislature to rescind the MCAS-passing requirement.

Those who advocated retaining the graduation requirement also knew that additional resources would be essential to provide students with the support necessary to learn and meet the English language arts and mathematics standards. The state commissioner of education made a strong case for providing districts with additional funds based on the number of students in the class of 2003 who had not passed both MCAS tests in the tenth grade. He was very clear that the goal for all students was to meet the rigorous standards and pass the MCAS tests. Fifty million dollars were allocated to school districts to provide additional time and learning for students in the class of 2003.

In Boston, where the stakes were highest because it schooled the largest number and percentage of students who had not passed the MCAS, the community was split within racial groups on what action to take. In Boston, the mayor, appointed school committee (school board), and I supported the action of the state commissioner of education and the State Board of Education to provide additional funding for the school districts with the highest concentrations of students who had not passed the MCAS tests. These funds enabled BPS to provide double time blocks of instruction in English language arts and mathematics for the class of 2003 to pass the MCAS and graduate on time. By June 2003, the percentage of seniors who passed both MCAS tests and met their course requirements increased to almost 80 percent. By the fall, those who completed additional summer school courses and passed the tests pushed the class of 2003 graduation rate to 80 percent.

How did this happen? There were a variety of contributing factors. The state provided additional resources to fund the essential support for the class of 2003 students to learn and develop the necessary skills to pass the demanding tests. Both tests contain a mix of multiple-choice and open-response questions. The English language arts test requires students to compose a prompt-driven long essay and write answers to open-response questions from reading comprehension passages. The mathematics test also requires students to show their work for some of the problems and explain why they decided to solve them that way. MCAS tests are created new each year. The data from the previous years' tests are available for teachers and students to review. The tests are aligned with standards, but there is no way to predict which standards will be assessed on a particular test. Teachers also have access to the students' essays from the prior years' tests.

Principals selected their most successful teachers to teach the double blocks of English language arts and mathematics. The school district also offered summer school programs. One unique program was called Classroom in the Workplace, which provided both summer jobs and additional academic support for high school students who had not passed MCAS tests. Employers agreed to provide space at the workplace for the students to spend the first ninety minutes of their work day with Boston Public School teachers, who helped them improve their literacy and math skills. The school district paid the teachers for their work, and the employers paid the students for a full eight-hour workday. Students who needed to earn money during the summer did not have to forgo employment to participate in an academic support program. Employers reinforced the importance of education in developing skills required for employment. Another important factor was the support and encouragement of the teachers union to get experienced, successful teachers to teach the double-block periods during the school year and classes at the workplaces of the students during the summer, even though the teachers union did not support the legislature's MCAS-passing policy as a graduation requirement and worked hard, but unsuccessfully, to change the law.

This experience provided evidence that it is possible to narrow achievement gaps, as demonstrated by the dramatic improvement of the BPS class of 2003 graduation rate. This experience also reinforced the sense of urgency to address the achievement gaps in a more systemic way and to develop strategies for narrowing the gaps, beginning with early childhood education and continuing through every level of elementary and secondary education. In addition to the gaps defined by racial groups, there are achievement gaps between special education students and English language learners and regular education students. Socioeconomic and gender achievement gaps also exist. The focus had been and continues to be on the gap between where students are and where they ought to be in achieving proficiency. In this situation, the goal was set for all students to meet the MCAS tests' proficiency standards. Strategies to meet this challenge included measuring and monitoring student progress, using data and research-based instructional strategies, increasing student attendance, providing professional development for teachers that was aligned with their work in the classroom, empowering parents, and promoting early literacy.

The school committee held community forums to engage parents and other community people in discussions about the achievement gaps and how the school district and community could work together to narrow them. A community coalition formed to address the challenges and keep the pressure on the superintendent and school committee. I created three subgroups within my leadership team to lead the work on the general achievement gaps and the gaps specific to English language learners and students with special needs. The framework with the essentials of whole-school improvement shaped both the district and school plans.

Strategies to Close Achievement Gaps

- **Acknowledge that achievement gaps exist and affirm our commitment to closing them.**

  Approach: Identify the scope of the challenge and declare it a top, urgent priority in every classroom of every school.

- **Establish and maintain high standards and expectations across the board.**

Approach: All adults and students must act on the belief that every student is capable of achieving at high levels. Require professional development for all staff in every school focused on high expectations for student learning.

- **Take a whole-school approach to closing the gap.** All students, staff, and parents must be integrated into the school's culture and its improvement strategies. Teachers and students in regular education, special education, and English language learner classrooms must be held to the same standards and expectations.

    Approach: Include regular education, special education, and English language learner staff in school instructional leadership teams, whole-school improvement plans, and collaborative coaching and learning and other professional development activities.

- **Support principals in leading the work.** The school leader is key to setting the tone and raising expectations of all members of the school community.

    Approach: Focus the summer institute and other professional development for all principals on strategies to close the achievement gap, including raising expectations and academic rigor, replicating best practices, engaging families and the community, and fostering racial and cultural competence.

- **Engage families and the community.** Schools alone cannot close the gap. Classroom learning must be reinforced at home and in the community. Schools, parents, higher education institutions, community-based organizations, and others must work together to address students' full range of academic and social needs.

Approach: Prioritize family and community engagement strategies to improve communication with families, involve parents in student learning, create family-friendly schools through effective school-family-community partnerships, and restructure family resource centers to better engage and support family participation.

- **Use a variety of assessments to measure student progress and improve the quality of instruction.** Test results and classroom work help educators understand what students are learning and not learning and also which instructional practices are more successful than others.

  Approach: Ongoing measurement of student learning is necessary through formative assessments, classroom work, and end-of-year test results. Ongoing assessment of student work by teachers in their classrooms and during common planning time with colleagues will help identify progress and gaps. Ongoing reflection on and modification of teaching practice will strengthen instruction.

- **Equip teachers with a variety of instructional strategies to address the broad range of student learning styles and needs.** Instruction must be adapted to student abilities and support the progression to higher levels of achievement.

  Approach: Provide scaffolding for students to build their confidence and belief in their ability to improve their work. Provide the appropriate materials for them to succeed at each level of their development and be ready with the stretch assignments and support that will help them to learn and achieve at the next level.

- **Change belief systems by demonstrating evidence of success.** Professional development must focus on best practices that raise expectations by proving that success is possible for all.

  Approach: Identify teachers who are improving the achievement of students who others doubt are capable of doing so. Have other teachers visit the classrooms of the successful teachers, look at student test results, and observe examples of effective teaching. Evidence can change beliefs and give doubters examples of how to improve their teaching.

- **Foster a school climate that is positive, safe, and nurturing.** Classrooms and school buildings must be supportive learning environments that are welcoming and respectful to students, staff, and families.

  Approach: Use school climate surveys to give students and staff the opportunity to assess important variables that affect success in classrooms and schools. Surveys should focus on such areas as school environment, student-teacher relationships, student-student relationships, and adult-adult relationships.

- **Identify students at greatest risk of failure and provide them with additional instruction time.**

  Approach: Maximize instruction time in literacy and mathematics through transition services as students move from level to level. Provide supplemental programs for out-of-school time during the summer and other breaks in the school calendar. Complete, implement, and monitor individual student support plans (ISSPs) for all students who have not achieved the standard of proficiency on the end-of-year assessments. Develop an online ISSP template to assist teachers in monitoring each student's plan.

- **Make classroom learning culturally relevant.** Curriculum and classroom activities must be relevant to a diverse urban population of predominantly low-income youth of color.

    Approach: Educators and others who work in school districts and schools with racial diversity must develop cultural competence. Adults should convey positive values and attitudes and model the behavior themselves if they expect students to learn what it means to be culturally competent, respect diversity of race and class, and honor the heritage of all students and adults in their school districts and schools.

- **Recruit, hire, and retain diverse teams of teachers and administrators.**

    Approach: Develop and implement intentional plans for recruiting, hiring, supporting, and retaining people of color, those who are bilingual and bicultural, and those who are certified special education educators as teachers, principals, and central office staff.

- **Secure and allocate appropriate resources for schools and classrooms based on the needs of students.** Leaders must have political courage and make the case for equity, which might require differentiated allocation of resources based on what is needed to ensure equal opportunity for all students to achieve.

    Approach: District and school leaders must engage in vigorous advocacy for the local, state, and federal resources necessary to ensure adequate funding. Careful monitoring of current resources that align the budget allocations with the priorities of the district and school education plans is essential. Obtaining partnerships with private foundations and businesses also is an important way for leaders to secure additional resources.

Narrowing and ultimately closing achievement gaps will continue to be a major challenge for urban school districts and schools. However, excuses for not knowing how to close the gaps are no longer acceptable. More examples of strategies are needed, and the ones that already exist need wider dissemination. One of my deputy superintendents in Boston, Dr. Ingrid Carney, supervised forty schools and was constantly reviewing data that revealed the need for targeted strategies to reverse the low achievement of black and Latino males and reduce the number of dropouts. She had a simple idea, which she called the Ten Boys Initiative for Closing the Achievement Gap. Schools identified cohorts of 10 boys in grades 3–11 with low achievement and set a goal for them to reach proficiency. Principal leadership, academic support, social and emotional support, leadership opportunities, and parent engagement were the focus of her strategies. After one year of implementation with 380 boys from grades 3–11 and thirty-eight schools, the results were impressive.

- 110 percent increase in the number of boys scoring proficient or advanced in English language arts, from 16.7 percent to 35 percent

- 123 percent increase in the number of boys scoring proficient or advanced in mathematics, from 12.3 percent to 27.4 percent

- 368 percent increase in the number of tenth-grade boys scoring proficient or advanced in mathematics, from 11.8 percent to 55.2 percent

- In year two, the Ten Boys Initiative expanded to include nearly a thousand boys, and it continues as an important program in BPS; it has generated interest in other school districts as well.

Special Education

School districts throughout the United States serve students with special needs through a variety of programs. Urban school districts and schools often have a higher percentage of students in special education programs than suburban or rural districts because cities also have medical care and other services children with disabilities require. Federal law (Education of All Handicapped Act, 1974) requires all states to adopt policies that guide and hold school districts responsible for educating students with disabilities. All fifty states now use the federal definitions for different types of disabilities, which range from mild to severe in each category. Federal legislation requires school districts and schools to provide every child who has a disability with a free and appropriate education beginning at the age of three and continuing until the student's twenty-second birthday. The language in federal legislation that promised funding to cover 40 percent of the cost of special education in states and school districts has not been honored. Thus, states and school districts have had to absorb most of the costs to provide quality special education programs and services for students. On average, 12 percent of the students in public schools have disabilities and require individual education plans (IEPs) tailored to address them. It is not unusual for urban school districts to have higher percentages. The percentage of district budgets dedicated to special education programs ranges from 10 to more than 20 percent.

Standards-based reform did not leave students with disabilities or English language learners behind. Special education students and English language learners also are required to take annual state tests. States may provide accommodations that address the needs of students with severe disabilities. However, many students in special education programs are capable of meeting the same high standards that students in general education must meet. Moreover, there are many students who have struggled with reading or mathematics and who have been referred in their early childhood years to special education to address their learning needs because their challenges could not be addressed in the regular classroom, and parents were lured by the promise of small classes and teacher expertise in special education. Students with challenging behavior, which in many instances could be addressed successfully in the regular classroom, are prematurely referred for special education. Once placed in special education programs, they are unlikely to return to the regular classroom. This practice has led to an overrepresentation of black and Latino males in special education programs in many urban school districts and schools.

Making more informed decisions about when to keep students in general education and when to refer students for special education assessment can make a positive difference. Early childhood education and primary school teachers are often the first teachers to make referrals. They should be trained with their principals on what criteria to use in making referrals and on other options to address student needs in the regular classroom before the referrals are made. Response to Intervention (RTI) allows teachers to use individual student data to assess whether or not what they have taught has been learned and what approaches they should use. Accommodations can be made that result in individual student improvement and fewer referrals to special education.

Inclusion classrooms or schools are another strategy for educating special education and general education students together. Typically the model requires two teachers, one who is licensed for special education and the other who has certification for the grade level or subjects being taught. Some districts have supported teachers and provided incentives for them to get dual certification. This model requires differentiated instruction and also provides the opportunity for whole-class instruction with a mixed group of students who can learn from each other. It helps eliminate the barriers that often exist in schools and classrooms when students are isolated from each other and thereby denied opportunities to learn and achieve at levels beyond what they may believe is attainable.

A third strategy focuses on students whose IEPs require them to be placed in private day or residential school settings because the public school district does not offer programs to meet their needs. The costs are substantially more than what local school districts would spend if they could offer programs of equal or better quality. In 1995 when I began my work as superintendent of BPS, there were 929 special education students in private-school placements at an average annual cost of about $65,000 a year. The average cost for students in the school district classrooms was $30,000 per year. I hired a new director of special education who was eager to start new, higher-quality BPS programs for day students. This was controversial and resisted by some parents. Once the new programs started in Boston, the school district began winning disputes about placements, and parents began to recognize the quality of the new programs the school district was able to provide. By 2008 there were only 370 students in private-school placements, with annual savings of $20 million, which then could be reallocated to improve instruction for all students. School districts have the responsibility to provide the necessary training for principals to ensure that they know how to embrace and support special education programs in the following situations:

- In substantially separate classrooms for special education students
- In full-inclusion models with a mix of regular and special education students
- In models with special education students being placed mainly in the regular classroom and spending some portion of the day outside with a special education teacher

- In models with the teacher providing support for the special education students by coming into the regular classroom

District leadership must attend to special education programs and embrace the commitment that the standards-based framework sets for all children to succeed. A supportive central office can make a positive difference. With a talented new director of special education in BPS, we were able to establish a new organizational unit called Unified Student Services, which included support staff who provided services for students with and without disabilities. Health, guidance, counseling, alternative education, and adult education services were offered as well as partnerships with community-based organizations such as community health centers and social service agencies. All students' needs were better met by including central office staff with skills and responsibilities in these support areas to help community-based organizations coordinate their services with those offered by the district. Coordination of services is never easy, but it is an essential goal that district and school leaders must adopt to address the diverse needs of students in districts and schools.

Student support teams were established at the school level. The high schools and middle schools had full-time student support coordinators; part-time coordinators were assigned to the elementary schools. The teams included the principal, several classroom teachers, and other staff, such as nurses, student support coordinators, and counselors. The focus of the meetings was to review the needs of students in the school and determine which ones required specific plans or modifications to plans already in place, and to determine whether one of the community-based partners should be engaged to provide the services defined by the plan. My team leader for Unified Student Services and I wrote a handbook based on our experience with the unified student services model (*Districts on the Move: Unified Student Service in Boston*

Public Schools: Building a Continuum of Services Through Standards-Based Reform, National Institute for Urban School Improvement, Arizona State University, Tempe, 2001).

The handbook provides eight lessons learned from implementing both "organizational and conceptual changes to unify models of service delivery":

- *Lesson 1*: Make sure that special education is working well when a unified model is launched.

- *Lesson 2*: Explicitly state and demonstrate the school district's intent to continue to build capacity to meet the needs of students with disabilities in the least restrictive environment.

- *Lesson 3*: Talk the reorganization through with all stakeholders.

- *Lesson 4*: Engage staff in creating unified models of service delivery at the school level.

- *Lesson 5*: Provide a user-friendly document that explains the unified model.

- *Lesson 6*: Talk unified and walk unified.

- *Lesson 7*: Make explicit connections between resources and unified support to schools.

- *Lesson 8*: Be vigilant in reviewing ongoing work through the lens of a unified model.

English Language Learners

During my tenure as superintendent of San Diego City Schools from 1982 to 1993, the school district had a significant increase in the number of English language learners. Most were immigrants from different countries, with the largest numbers arriving from Mexico and other countries in Central and South America.

In addition, families from Vietnam, Cambodia, Laos, Somalia, and other countries had San Diego as their destination. They ended up in different parts of the city and registered at public schools where the school district was able to provide transitional bilingual education programs. These programs began with instruction in the students' native languages, followed by increasing time focused on English instruction; they ultimately led to transitioning to full-time English-speaking classrooms. Expectations varied among the families of the various language groups. Some expected the schools to teach their children to read and write in both the native languages and English. Others wanted the schools to focus on English only, and the families expected to take responsibility at home for maintaining their native languages.

The biggest challenge was finding qualified bilingual teachers. It was easier to find and hire qualified teachers who were fluent in English and Spanish, and more difficult to do so with the other languages. Monitoring the transitions from dual-language instruction to English only revealed disparities among language groups in the number of years it took for students to transition from bilingual programs to regular English classes. We also learned more about why the expectations were different among the language groups. Some years after I left San Diego, the State of California offered a proposition requiring English-only programs for teaching English language learners. The proposition passed and set the stage for other states with growing populations of immigrants from different countries to consider similar ballot measures. In 2002 an English-only measure was placed on the ballot in Massachusetts, and to the surprise of many it passed easily. At the time there were eight transitional bilingual programs offered in BPS that had to be eliminated and replaced by sheltered English-only programs. Sheltered English programs require that students meet rigorous standards. However, although the standards remain high, the pace of instruction is adjusted to use the best techniques for teaching a second language in a sheltered environment. The goal is to move students within eighteen months into regular classrooms with teachers who may or may not have training in teaching English language learners with various levels of proficiency in English. This quickly creates a challenge to provide new training and support for all teachers in the school district. Regular classroom teachers must acquire the skills necessary to teach students who are still at various levels of English proficiency. This effort must be systemic and continued from year to year because of teacher turnover. In short, a multiple-year effort is required.

Districts across the country are responding to this challenge with a variety of strategies. Some states are adding certification requirements for teachers to get training in how to teach English language learners. Districts may offer pay incentives to attract teachers with the skills necessary to teach this population. Systemwide professional development for all teachers is another option, but it is very expensive and difficult to offer at scale in a single year. RTI strategies, which have been effective in special education, are being tried with English language learners, with evidence of success. States with high concentrations of English language learners often require teacher training institutions to include courses and field experience in schools as part of the requirements of their programs and ultimately certification.

Certainly demand for teachers with dual certification is increasing and adds another dimension to the skill set that district and school leaders must acquire. The disaggregation of test results for subgroups such as special education and English language learners required by the No Child Left Behind (NCLB) federal legislation shined a bright spotlight on these two groups of students, who were often forgotten when test results were discussed. Accountability for educators to educate all children to higher standards changed the conversation, and the disaggregation of data provided the evidence to help them do so. Now the availability of additional data provides more clarity about meeting the needs of children with a wide range of disabilities and more of a consensus among educators on how to do so. Leaders in schools and school districts are still considering how to implement strategies to meet the needs of English language learners. One of the promising models is the dual-language programs in which native English-speaking students and native Spanish-speaking students begin kindergarten together in a program designed to develop fluency for both groups in both languages. However, English language learners enroll in schools at every grade level, which requires leaders in school districts and schools to develop additional programs to meet their needs.

The expectations to improve all student achievement have challenged those who may believe that separate standards may be necessary for some students to experience success. However, the data and expectation that states assess special education students and English language learners have shown evidence of successfully closing gaps. This reinforces the importance of having evidence to convince doubters that all students, even those who have been characterized as unable to achieve at progressively higher levels, are indeed able to do so with the right support. District and school leaders must lead by example and demonstrate by their actions that they value diversity in their districts and schools and welcome the challenge to do whatever it takes to make sure that English language learners and students with disabilities have the support they need to succeed, meet high standards, and graduate from high school ready for some kind of continuing education.

Leading from the Middle

Throughout this book, the focus has been on leaders who lead from the top in school districts and schools—superintendents and principals. There are many other leaders in the central office; they report to the superintendent's four to six direct reports, and provide services and support to the principals and schools. They are leading from the middle of the organization and are trying to meet the needs of the school and honor the priorities established by the board, superintendent, and senior leadership staff. Sometimes the schools' expectations for support cannot be met because they clash with those leading from the top. When this occurs, the leaders in the middle are often blamed by those in the schools for failing to respond to and meet their requests. The dissonance that may result must be addressed immediately by the superintendent and senior leadership team, or the commitment to develop coherence in the school district and alignment of duties and responsibilities at all levels will be compromised. School boards select superintendents and hold them accountable for implementing the policies they adopt. They too lead from the top, but in most cases, elected officials listen to constituents and consider recommendations from the superintendent before they make policy decisions.

Most school district employees are assigned to schools, and their contact with central office staff is sporadic. Contact with the HR department is necessary during the initial hiring process, and perhaps a payroll problem requires a teacher or other school staff member to call or visit the payroll office. Central office employees from procurement, maintenance, custodial, transportation, and other operations departments do have more direct contact with schools than other central office employees. Leaders of those departments typically go to schools to deal with emergencies. In some large school districts, the chief financial officer will assign budget office employees to work with groups of schools to offer better access and quicker response to principals who are seeking assistance. They all work in the middle of the organization and are critical employees who are responsible for the operation of the district and schools.

School districts also have many central office leaders who provide services and support for teaching and learning, curriculum and instruction. In addition, there are those who supervise principals. In urban school districts, common leadership personnel who directly report to the superintendent include chief academic officer, deputy superintendent, chief operating officer, chief communications officer, chief financial officer, and chief of staff. Some superintendents prefer to have five or six direct reports; others may have ten or more. The position of chief academic officer (CAO) has become popular in recent years in many large districts. There are two models. In one model the CAO oversees the work that focuses on teaching and learning, such as curriculum and instruction, special education, English language learners, counseling, health, professional development, research, assessment and evaluation, and other departments that support the core teaching and learning work. The central office leaders that address these program areas are the CAO's direct reports. A second model increases the CAO's span of control by including as direct reports those who supervise the principals.

My own experience is that there is no one-size-fits-all organizational design that uniformly defines who should be the direct reports to the superintendent. These staff function as the first tier of leaders who are challenged with leading from the middle. Hiring people who have the requisite skills for senior leadership positions and report directly to the superintendent has always been my priority. Often this required modifications in the design of the organization. When I was with BPS, my practice was to have a separate meeting each week with my senior leadership team, which included three deputy superintendents who supervised principals, a deputy superintendent for teaching and learning, a deputy superintendent for family and community engagement, a chief operating officer, and a chief of staff. An expanded leadership team met for two hours every other week. I included the ten principals who were also cluster leaders and several other central office leaders, such as the chief financial officer; assistant superintendent for human resources; and director of research, assessment, and evaluation. These leaders were those who had responsibility for staff who truly had to lead from the middle.

These meetings were beneficial because I learned what the significant issues were and what challenges these leaders were facing, and how the central office staff who were assigned to work with the schools were addressing them. And when I met with the principals I could get their views on the quality of central office support. If there were mixed messages, I would present them to my senior leadership team and assign the appropriate members responsibility for resolving them. There are a number of challenges for those who lead from the middle. Leaders serving at all levels in school districts struggle when there is a lack of clarity about their roles and responsibilities. Departments in school district offices often function as silos where staff focus only on their own work and lobby for additional resources to address their expanding workload. Others are protectionists hanging on to what has always been, fearful of changes in focus and tasks that might result in the elimination of existing jobs due to new technology.

Urban public schools in the United States periodically have faced cycles of growth supported by new revenue from local, state, and federal sources and from major foundations that have funded reform strategies. And we have survived difficult downturns in the economy. During fiscal years 2003 and 2004, budget cuts in BPS totaled $85 million with seven hundred positions eliminated from the school district, of which four hundred were teaching positions. Currently school district budgets are being developed for the 2010–11 school year and beyond, with deep cuts from previous years continuing but insufficient to balance future budgets. With 80 percent or more of district budgets allocated for salaries and benefits, few school district budgets can be balanced without eliminating positions. Understandably superintendents and principals will attempt to keep the cuts away from schools and classrooms if they can. The pressure from many inside the school district as well as external stakeholders is to cut positions held by the people who lead from the middle at the central office first because they are unknown to many in the schools and therefore unappreciated.

Difficult budget situations can create an opportunity for district leaders to change the traditional culture of the central office and work with principals to do the same in schools. Some ways to change the culture in schools were discussed in previous chapters, and they require training and support for principals to lead the efforts. Principals are the most important leaders in the middle. They are pushed and pulled on the one hand by their school staffs, parents, and community members, and on the other hand by those in the central office who lead from the middle as well. The first district I led as superintendent had only eight schools and 4,500 students; the principals were my direct reports. And even though there were 22,000 students in the second district; 45,000 in the third district; 125,000 in the fourth district; and 64,000 in my fifth district, Boston, I never had more than one layer of leadership between me and the principals. (And, as noted earlier, ten principals served on my expanded leadership team in Boston.) I met with them periodically in large and small groups and got to know them by making three to four unannounced visits to schools each week. My connection to the principals made it much easier for them to lead from the middle. However, at times it created tensions between other central office leaders in the middle, who believed they should have been dealing directly with the principals rather than with the superintendent doing so.

As a superintendent, it was always difficult to create a balance between the attention I gave to central office leaders in the middle and those in the schools. It was easy to find fault with the culture of isolation and competition that exists in the central office when the superintendent fails to lead the trust-building effort and find ways to open up the office silos. Without taking steps to do so, it is difficult to build a coherent organization with a clear sense of purpose. It is easy to keep repeating the words, "The central office exists to serve the schools." However, the view from the schools is often, "The central office exists to tell us what to do, and when it attempts to help us, it usually misses the mark."

The following are some suggestions of what superintendents can do to help the central office staff:

- The superintendent should visit the departments in the central office periodically and meet with the leaders to seek their advice, receive and share information, review data, and discuss priorities. Unannounced short, informal visits to central office departments without an entourage are great morale boosters.

- The superintendent can devise a collaborative project that brings together a cross section of central office and school staff to tackle a major district challenge. The appointment of the project manager is critical. The project manager must be a team builder, facilitator, taskmaster, collaborator, and respected colleague who understands that the composite work of the whole team will yield better results than individuals working alone could produce. Moreover, there is accountability for results. This collaboration can dispel stereotypes and lead to a better understanding of each other's departments.

- The superintendent can endorse reciprocal visit days two or three times each year. The design is simple. A principal spends a day in a central office department, working together with the central office employees. Central office employees visit a school and spend the entire day with the principal learning about the tasks, challenges, and surprises that principals encounter in a typical day. It was amazing to me to learn that many principals and central office staff had for years conversed by telephone and never met each other.

- The superintendent can attend professional development programs, which often are held at the central office. Opening the session with greetings, the super-intendent can point to the importance of the group's work and how it aligns with the priorities of the school district.

- The superintendent could try innovative solutions, which might be viewed negatively by some leaders and other employees in the school district. Outsourcing some central support functions could lead to reductions in costs and increases in quality of services. School districts with unions may face great resistance to such propos-als. Some of that resistance may be reduced by requiring vendors to employ some of the school district employees who lose their jobs. The discussion of outsourcing could result in existing internal teams perhaps creating propos-als that could beat those of outside providers.

The superintendent must model behavior that is expected of others and not communicate only through written memos. Connecting to leaders in the middle in their settings gives the superintendent a better understanding of their work and how they do it. Presence is important. That is why regular unannounced school visits should not be trumped by an inflexible schedule that results in ten- to twelve-hour days in the office.

No organization can achieve coherence without clarity about priorities and alignment of the strategies used to implement them. Few organizations can succeed without capable people lead-ing from the middle. They will be judged by the schools and the superintendent on the results of their leadership.

Federal and State Roles

It is not the purpose of this book to review how federal and state governments have affected public education. However, it is impor-tant to understand their roles in setting policy, providing funding, and holding districts and schools accountable for results. Early in 2010, President Obama and Secretary of Education Arne Duncan made clear their intentions to seek congressional reauthorization of the Elementary and Secondary Education Act (ESEA) by the end of the year. For forty-five years this act has been the major source of federal funding for elementary and secondary schools, with a focus on schools that serve high concentrations of students from low-income families. The expectation is that there will be significant changes in NCLB legislation, which was passed with bipartisan support in both houses of Congress in late 2001 and was signed into law by President George W. Bush in early 2002. Sections of that law created ongoing controversy. The accountability system was driven by the expectation that all students would reach proficiency by 2014 on the required end-of-year state tests for grades 4, 8, and 10. There were fifty different sets of standards for reading and mathematics and fifty different state tests. The result was significant variation from state to state in the standards and the rigor of the curriculum and the end-of-year tests. School districts and schools in each state were judged by the annual test results and the amount of improvement made each year. If the improvement was not sufficient for the school district and individual schools to make adequate yearly progress to achieve the 2014 goal of all students reaching proficiency, the legislation included sanctions that increased in severity with each consecutive year the annual targets were not reached. School districts and schools were judged based on the performance of all students and the performance of subgroups defined by gender, race, disabilities, language, and free and reduced-price lunch eligibility. The bipartisan support for the legislation approved in 2001 was garnered in part by the promise that substantial increases in federal funding for qualifying school districts and schools would be forthcoming. Although the appropriations for NCLB were increased, the amounts fell far short of what had been proposed, and the promise for significant additional funding was broken.

The bipartisan support for the legislation in its early years of implementation also led to bipartisan criticism of its shortcomings. The presidential campaign and most of the congressional campaigns in 2008 did not treat federal education policy as a major issue. But it was an issue that did get some traction with the expectation that it would be on the next tier of priorities after the economy, jobs, wars in the Middle East, and health care were addressed first. There is hope that ESEA will be reauthorized again soon.

In 2009 and 2010, the federal government's stimulus funds positively affected many states and school districts for the short term. However, it is always problematic to use one-time money for recurring costs. President Obama is proposing a significant increase in education funding for 2011, even though he also is proposing cuts in a number of other domestic programs. In 2010, the U.S. Department of Education program Race to the Top will provide funding to a small number of states that must compete by submitting applications that show plans for innovation and improvement in student achievement and closing achievement gaps. However, these grants are going to only a few states and will not solve what is a continuing funding problem in most states. To answer this concern, Secretary Duncan has proposed that individual school districts will be able to submit applications for the 2011 Race to the Top programs to help create sustainable systemic reform. He also is requesting additional funding to help reinstate teachers who have been laid off due to the recession and cuts in state and local funds for school districts.

States have a significant responsibility in setting policy and funding public education, but there is wide variation among the states in the policies they set, the funding they provide, and their accountability systems. State legislatures and governors have major roles in determining how state dollars are allocated to school districts and schools for operating and capital budgets. Collective bargaining rights for public employees are established by state policy, but not in right-to-work states. Certification and licensure requirements for educators who work in public school districts and schools are approved by state boards of education and state departments of education led by superintendents of public instruction or education commissioners. States are required by federal legislation to develop standards for curriculum, setting expectations for what students should know and be able to do in various subjects and in different grade levels. They also have responsibility for developing and scoring the annual state tests required by federal policy. Typically this work is outsourced.

Another responsibility of the states is to hold school districts and schools accountable for carrying out state and federal policy that cover such areas as special education, English language learners, and low-performing schools and school districts. Review teams are convened by the state departments of education and sent into school districts and schools to determine whether they are in compliance with state policy and regulations. These reviews require district and school leaders to prepare extensive reports for the visiting team that include data on all aspects of the district and schools' work. Some states have legislation that gives the state the authority to take over low-performing districts or schools or require them to bring in leaders who are capable of turning them around.

Many states provide funding for competitive grants in targeted areas. For example, in 2006 Massachusetts created a grant competition for urban middle schools interested in extending the students' school day by several hours. This provided an opportunity for students who would benefit from double periods of English language arts and mathematics without sacrificing their ability to take elective programs in art, music, physical education, dance, theater, and other areas. Teachers were not required to work through the extended day. This gave the three middle schools in Boston who won grants the opportunity to form partnerships with community-based organizations that provided a variety of art, music, physical education, drama, writing, and other programs that could not be offered during the regular school day. They also provided some teachers who could work with students in the elective programs. Three years of data showed that attendance was up, student grades were improving, and the partnerships with community-based organizations and the extended-day middle schools were demonstrating how effective new partnerships can be.

Conclusion

Leading in a complex environment is not easy. Difficult times will continue to require school district and school leaders to make difficult choices and determine how to leverage budget reductions to align resources with their educational plans. They still will struggle to change culture from one dominated by adults to one focused on students. School district and school leaders must show staff how to embrace collaboration and teamwork. It will require changing systems to schedule planning time, creating structures and tasks for teams to work together, and visiting schools to learn best practices that are producing gains in student achievement and narrowing achievement gaps. Embracing opportunity when it is present and creating it when it is not are what innovative and successful leaders do. It is the people at all levels in the school district, but especially the teachers and principals, who must provide the quality of instruction and leadership necessary to educate students well in all schools.

School district and school leaders rarely get through a day without surprises, no matter how well prepared they are to deal with the unknown. We all know people who are dissatisfied with their jobs. And there are examples in every organization of a poor fit between the leader and the particular job. Leaders do have good days and bad days. However, successful leaders are resilient. Each knows that it is better to fall asleep the minute his or her head hits the pillow than fret and revisit in his or her mind the day just concluded. A leader who starts the day exhausted will not have a good day and will lose ground in cultivating the relationships necessary to motivate all who must be partners in the leadership work. The wonderful constant for leaders is coming to work every day knowing that they will never be bored.

Even in good times, leading urban school districts and schools is also challenging and difficult. Leaders must lead in a public fish bowl, where transparency is expected and must be embraced by superintendents and principals and those who lead from the middle. Transparency challenges and should trump the elements of school culture that eschew sharing, collaborative learning, and the use of data to better understand what is working for students first and adults second. Leaders of complex organizations are constantly in motion, adapting each day to the unanticipated while pushing their agenda of doing a few things well rather than many things superficially. They are driven by their commitment to provide an education for all students that will provide them with access to opportunity when they graduate from high school. Leaders understand that people are the most valuable asset that they must develop and protect.

7

Conclusion

The focus of this book has been to set forth the various dimensions of leadership and the ways that successful leaders make a positive difference in urban school districts and schools. The premise is that leaders must know not only what to do but also how to do it. Setting goals is important, developing strategies for meeting the goals is essential, and knowing how to do the necessary work to get the desired results is critical. Compartmentalization of these components will diminish the odds for achieving desired results, whereas alignment of the components to a coherent set of expectations for achieving improved teaching and learning can lead to positive outcomes for all children.

Standards-based reform has provided a framework for what components must be included in aligned, coherent plans to help all students reach higher standards. It is much easier to provide descriptions of the characteristics successful leaders have than to provide exact details about how to get the desired results. Each chapter addresses the question of what leaders should do and provides examples of what has worked.

Characteristics of Leaders

Whether leaders are born with leadership skills or whether these skills can be learned has been debated for a long time. In my experience, aspiring leaders can learn the leadership skills necessary to be effective. However, some of the characteristics of leadership listed here require self-reflection, continuous learning, and additional experience. This list of characteristics reflects my own experience. Most of them are applicable to many leaders regardless of the type of organizations and sectors they lead. A few characteristics of leadership may be unique and defined by the sector in which the organization exists.

Characteristics of School District and School Leaders

- Leaders must know who they are, what their strengths and weaknesses are, and how others view them.

- Leaders must model the behavior they expect others in the organization to model.

- Leaders must be thick skinned but not insensitive.

- Leaders must eschew the "leader says" culture by giving permission to others to talk freely with them.

- Leaders must be great listeners and provide constructive feedback to acknowledge what they have heard and how they are going to use the information.

- Leaders must respect all of the employees in the organization regardless of their statuses or roles.

- Leaders must have a moral sense of right and wrong without being moralistic.

- Leaders must build relationships that convey transparency and integrity.

- Leaders must distribute leadership and build high-functioning teams.

- Leaders must embrace diversity in the workplace and provide the opportunity for all employees to increase their understanding of issues concerning gender, race, class, language, and disability to build a culture of collaboration.

- Leaders must convey to all that hiring the right people for the appropriate positions is the most important decision made in the organization.

- Leaders must have knowledge of the organization's core work to lead the improvement of teaching and learning for all students.

- Leaders must be clear about the distinctions between equal and equitable decisions and willing to differentiate the allocations of resources accordingly.

- Leaders must be transparent about the organization's accountability system, the standards for performance in the organization, and the metrics and data used to assess results.

- Leaders must be authentic communicators who can connect with many different audiences in a variety of venues and in good and bad times.

- Leaders must be forthcoming and clear when mistakes are made, take responsibility for the organization's performance, and show that steps will be taken to ensure that the mistakes will not be repeated.

- Leaders must have a keen sense of what should be sustained and what must be changed and improved in the organization to realize desired results.

Frameworks and Strategies for Improving Student Achievement

The challenge for leaders in urban school districts and schools is to adopt systemic thinking and effectively use systemic strategies to improve student achievement in every school and classroom. Having a few more good schools in the school district or a few more good classrooms in every school is not sufficient to meet the goal of educating all students properly. What follows are lists summarizing some key successful frameworks, strategies, and actions to improve student achievement and narrow and close achievement gaps. The common theme is that there must be alignment among the strategies. It is essential for leaders to understand the importance of ensuring coherence with the work. The frameworks and strategies listed here do not have a priority order, and leaders will not use them all at the same time. However, they should contribute to the coherence and alignment of the overall district or school plan.

Standards-Based Reform Framework

- Create clear standards that set expectations for what students should know and be able to do.

- Make sure all teachers and learners have access to a rigorous curriculum aligned with the standards.

- Provide support for teachers and school leaders to continually learn how to improve the quality of instruction in the classroom and leadership in school districts and schools.

- Offer transparent accountability systems that include qualitative indicators describing the characteristics of effective teaching and leadership, and quantitative indicators based on student achievement data.

Seven Essentials of the Whole-School Improvement Framework

- The Core Essential: Effective Instruction
- Student Work and Data
- Professional Development
- Shared Leadership
- Resources
- Families and Community
- Operational Excellence

Problem-Solving Approach to Strategy Design and Implementation[1]

- Identify the Problem
- Analyze the Problem and Diagnose Its Causes
- Develop a Theory of Action
- Design the Strategy
- Plan for Implementation
- Implement the Strategy
- Assess Progress
- Adapt and Modify for Continuous Improvement

Key Elements for the Design and Implementation of Systemic Reform Plans in Urban Schools

The following are important elements for leaders to address in the design of school district and school change and improvement plans:

Vision describes the destination—where the district or school wants to go.

Mission states what has to be accomplished for the destination to be reached.

Theory of action sets forth the specific expectations about how to get to the destination by stating that if we use a particular strategy and implement it with fidelity, we can expect to achieve a defined result.

Goals provide specific targets and timelines for results.

---

[1]Reprinted with permission from (PEL-064) "A Problem-Solving Approach to Designing and Implementing a Strategy to Improve Performance: Synopsis by Stacey Childress, Geoff Marrietta. Copyright © 2010 by the President and Fellows of Harvard College; all rights reserved.

Plans include the strategies that will be used to reach the goals and how the results will be measured.

Review of data is needed to determine the extent to which the goals have been reached and how to assess results.

Choice of Strategies

Selection of three to five systemic strategies for improving teaching and learning with allocation of the resources necessary to execute them with fidelity and in depth will result in better student achievement results than can be expected using multiple strategies and programs with fewer resources allocated.

Governance

Most school board members in the United States are elected. In recent years mayoral appointment of school board members has gained traction, particularly in some large urban school districts. Regardless of which model is used, continuity of leadership on school boards is an important variable and affects the opportunity for superintendents and other key leaders in school districts to serve long enough to see systemic change and improvement. The typical tenure of a large-city superintendent is three years, which is not enough time for a district leader to design and implement a reform and improvement plan and see significant improvement in student achievement. Since 2000, more continuity of leadership on school boards has resulted in more continuity of leadership for superintendents. And many of these districts have demonstrated significant improvement in student achievement and narrowing achievement gaps.

Human Capital

Recruiting, hiring, training, supporting, and retaining teachers, principals, superintendents, and other staff are critical to the improvement of urban school districts and schools. Systemic reform is successful when people with the right skills have leadership positions, focus on change and improvement, and drive the core leadership work. Human capital is the biggest challenge now facing public education in the United States, and it will continue to face us in the years ahead.

Culture

It is very difficult to change the existing culture in organizations. However, being able to do so is one of the skills that leaders need in order to improve school districts and schools. Collaboration is often the goal, but the systems and structures in schools, where teachers spend most of their day working alone in classrooms with students, make it difficult for teachers to work together in teams. This culture of isolation in schools is a barrier that prohibits colleagues' meeting together to learn from each other and discuss how to address problems of practice. In most sectors, professionals spend at least eight hours a day at their work locations, where real-time interaction and teamwork are expected and necessary. And many spend additional time in the workplace and take work home as well.

The new generation of teachers does not want to work in isolated classroom settings with a schedule that limits contact with colleagues and the opportunity to work in teams and learn from each other. If teachers and other school staff worked an eight-hour day and an eleven-month work year, opportunities for teamwork, professional development, and summer school programs would be extensive. Systems and structures could be redesigned to support a collaborative culture; compensation plans would require adjustment as well. Some of the additional costs would be offset by the elimination of stipends and extra pay currently required to compensate teachers for time they are asked to provide beyond the current school day.

Accountability

Although high-performing school districts and schools are making decisions that are data driven, proactive school districts and schools understand that accountability systems should not focus on test results alone. It is clear that the quality of the teaching is the key variable affecting student achievement. Educators must focus on what good instruction is, what it looks like in schools and classrooms, and how to support it by helping teachers improve their practice. It is necessary to build qualitative indicators into accountability systems and not rely on quantitative indicators alone.

Professional Development

There is little evidence to support the connection between the number of courses teachers take and the impact the courses have on the improvement of their teaching. The days carved out of the school calendar for professional development programs held in the school district while students stay home may have short-term payoff for teachers, but all too often they return to their classrooms without being able to see the connection between their teaching challenges and the professional development sessions they were required to attend. Embedding professional development at the school level, with the leadership of principals who have been trained as instructional leaders, holds promise for meeting the needs of teachers; this use of shared learning would also be a positive way to move the culture of the school toward collaboration.

———

Having all students graduate from high school ready without remediation for at least some postsecondary education is our essential goal. The states' engagement in the process of developing common standards, and assessments that align with them, is a breakthrough strategy that will drive reform in school districts and schools, and is essential to begin closing the "rigor gap" that exists between international standards in other industrialized nations and our standards in America.

Leadership matters. This book on leadership is designed to address the key questions district and school leaders must answer to succeed in improving the quality of education for all the students they serve. The key questions are What should I do? Why should I do it? How will I do it? What kind of evidence must I have to learn and understand what does and does not work? Answers to these questions based on my experience will, I hope, assist district and school leaders in becoming successful and enable them to make a positive difference in the education of the students they serve.

This challenging work is essential and achievable. Today's successful leaders in school districts and schools know that they must focus on both qualitative and quantitative evidence rather than just opinion to set goals, develop strategies, build capacity in people to do the work, measure results, and embrace continuous learning. School districts and schools can experience the positive effect that alignment and coherence can create. Good leaders can build high-performing organizations that will make a positive difference for all the children who are educated in U.S. urban school districts and schools.

Index

Titles in the Jossey-Bass
Leadership Library in Education Series

WOMEN AND EDUCATIONAL LEADERSHIP
Margaret Grogan and Charol Shakeshaft
• ISBN 978-0-4704-7043-5

URBAN SCHOOL LEADERSHIP
Tom Payzant • ISBN 978-0-7879-8621-6

TURNAROUND LEADERSHIP
Michael Fullan • ISBN 978-0-7879-6985-1

DISTRIBUTED LEADERSHIP
James P. Spillane • ISBN 978-0-7879-6538-9

INCLUSIVE LEADERSHIP
James Ryan • ISBN 978-0-7879-6508-2

SUSTAINABLE LEADERSHIP
Andy Hargreaves and Dean Fink • ISBN 978-0-7879-6838-0

ETHICAL LEADERSHIP
Robert J. Starratt • ISBN 978-0-7879-6564-8

TEACHER LEADERSHIP
Ann Lieberman and Lynne Miller • ISBN 978-0-7879-6245-6